LEARNING TEACHING

BECOMING AN INSPIRATIONAL TEACHER

PETE BOYD

BARRY HYMER

KAREN LOCKNEY

First published in 2015 by Critical Publishing Ltd
Reprinted in 2016 and 2017

The authors have made every effort to ensure the accuracy of information contained in this publication, but assume no responsibility for any errors, inaccuracies, inconsistencies and omissions. Likewise every effort has been made to contact copyright holders. If any copyright material has been reproduced unwittingly and without permission the Publisher will gladly receive information enabling them to rectify any error or omission in subsequent editions.

British Library Cataloguing in Publication Data
A CIP record for this book is available from the British Library

ISBN: 978-1-909682-45-0

This book is also available in the following e-book formats:

MOBI ISBN: 978-1-909682-46-7
EPUB ISBN: 978-1-909682-47-4
Adobe e-book ISBN: 978-1-909682-48-1

The rights of Pete Boyd, Barry Hymer and Karen Lockney to be identified as the Authors of this work have been asserted by them in accordance with the Copyright, Design and Patents Act 1988.

Cover design by Joe Boyd / Greensplash Limited
Text design by Greensplash Limited
Project Management by Out of House Publishing
Print managed and manufactured by Jellyfish Solutions

Critical Publishing
3 Connaught Road
St Albans
AL3 5RX
www.criticalpublishing.com

Paper from responsible sources

Contents

People are talking about this book ...

'Really got me thinking about my practice'

'Really, really liked the scenarios because I was able to relate to them ... been there!'

'The key questions and the discussions were excellent – it kind of modelled how I should reflect on my own lessons'

'It was provocative – I really like the invitation to be an activist questioning teacher'

'Made me want to try some new ideas'

'Things to try – really useful'

'I would like this book for my next placement'

'Very stimulating'

'Can we cite this book in our assignment?'

'I really want to get my hands on it'

'It's like someone talking to you'

Acknowledgements

This book is offered as a guide to help you find your way through the challenges and complexity of becoming the kind of teacher that really makes a difference to individual learners. The book is a collaborative project between the three authors, all formerly school teachers and now working in teacher education and development. Our thanks go, in particular, to the creative and inspirational teachers that we are privileged to work with, including those within our vibrant teacher education partnership at the University of Cumbria. The design of the book was inspired in part by Jonah Sachs's great book *Winning the Story Wars* and is an attempt to create an empowerment narrative to support the journey of becoming an inspirational teacher.

In practical terms we are grateful for advice and feedback from our publisher Julia Morris and to friends and colleagues who gave feedback on early drafts including Sarah Claxton, Christina Kennedy, Hazel Messenger, Iain Patterson, Anne Quinn, Suzanne Romney and Catherine Steel. In particular, we would like to thank Professor Hilary Constable for her careful review and annotation of a draft version of the book. Professor David Leat deserves a special mention for his thinking and questioning which has helped to shape this book. Thanks also to illustrator Joe Boyd for the cover design. We appreciate all feedback given by readers of our early drafts; any oversights or mistakes remain our own responsibility.

Pete Boyd, Barry Hymer and Karen Lockney, 2015

Meet the authors

Pete Boyd is Professor of Professional Learning at the University of Cumbria, UK. For the first 15 years of his career he taught in secondary schools, including a short period in a residential field study and outdoor education centre. Pete became a lecturer in teacher education and then moved into academic development work within the university. His day-to-day teaching and consultancy involves supporting teachers and lecturers to lead change in practice through their practitioner research projects. Pete's research and publications are focused on the identity and workplace learning of educators, the pedagogy of teacher education and assessment for learning. He is an outdoor enthusiast – mountaineer, rock-climber, skier and mountain-biker – and lives on the edge of the beautiful Lake District National Park in the north-west of England.

Barry Hymer is Professor of Psychology in Education at the University of Cumbria, England (part-time) and a freelance educational consultant and trainer. His background is as a primary and secondary school teacher and educational psychologist. Barry has particular interests and expertise in the related areas of motivation, mindset, talent development and independent learning. Barry has toured with Professor Carol Dweck, the originator of mindset theory, on several occasions, speaking at conferences in England and abroad. This is his ninth book, and the first aimed specifically at teachers in the early stages of their careers. Barry lives in a small Passivhaus on the banks of the River Lune near Lancaster, England, from which base he indulges his interests in cycling, walking, world cinema and chess.

Karen Lockney is a Senior Lecturer at the University of Cumbria, UK, and has taught on a variety of programmes relating to primary and secondary teacher education and the wider children's workforce. Prior to moving into higher education, Karen taught in secondary schools for ten years, spending the majority of these as a Head of English. Karen writes and publishes poetry, and her creative writing doctorate included a body of poems related to contemporary rural life in the Eden Valley in Cumbria. Her main research interests are the links between reading and writing in schools; literature for young people; place-based identity; and poetry pedagogy. Her research involves working collaboratively with pupils and teachers in classroom contexts. Karen is a regional consultant for Poetry by Heart, a national poetry recitation competition, and she is also a primary school governor. Karen lives at the foot of the North Pennines with her husband and daughter, and living in a farming community on the edge of a beautiful and empty landscape is something she very much enjoys.

You can contact the authors and publisher on Twitter:

Authors: **@learnteachbook**

Critical Publishing: **@CriticalPub**

Endorsement

It takes 10 years or more to begin to be a brain surgeon, but sometimes we get one to three years at most before we are allowed to work with children's brains as teachers. So we need inspirational teachers and this is the focus of this compact, powerful and insightful book. It is wonderfully designed around five of the most critical dilemmas in our classrooms: belief vs. ability; autonomy vs. compliance; abstract vs. concrete; feedback vs. praise; and collaboration vs. competition. The power of the book is that it illustrates the new move to focus on learning power – and such a focus permits every student to become smarter through effort and deep practice as they struggle with the high-challenge learning activities – in the presence of inspirational, impactful and passionate teachers. The perfect book for those who want to make the most of their opportunity to enhance students' brain power.

John Hattie
Director, Melbourne Education Research Institute
Laureate Professor, Melbourne Graduate School of Education
University of Melbourne

Chapter 1   Practical wisdom *and* public knowledge

*Brains are born, and minds are made; and one of the privileges of the teaching
profession is to have an important part to play in the shaping of minds.*
(Elliot W. Eisner, 1998, p 23)

Learning teaching

This book is not a straightforward 'how to teach' professional manual. It doesn't point you in
the direction of current national directives or offer a teaching-by-numbers 'tips for teachers'
guide. Nor does it offer any easy or quick route to professional competence and qualified
teacher status. We believe there is merit in many of the publications for beginning teachers,
offering sound advice based on established educational orthodoxies and would encourage
you to engage reflectively with such texts.

This book, however, is more of an additional or advanced critical reader; it is aimed at beginning teachers but we hope it may also be of interest to more experienced practitioners.
In writing the book we have made a few assumptions about your knowledge of the teaching basics. There is, after all, some consensus around the characteristics of well-planned,
effective teaching: the value of being present at the start of a lesson to receive and greet
your class as individuals and with respect, for instance, or the thoughtful development of
intended learning outcomes as a useful step in lesson planning. We recognise too that it can
be helpful to develop 'success criteria' and to share them with the learners so that they have
a better idea of what success in the learning task will look like. It also goes without saying
that following skilful introduction to a new idea, learners will benefit from guided practice,
during which they receive feedback to help improve their work. And further independent
practice is then important, especially when the learners have to apply new learning to solve
problems within a different context.

We don't labour these and some other points, but this does not mean we disregard them.
But even these educational verities are open to challenge: teaching is at least as much an
art as a science, and art holds open the potential for disrupting orthodoxy, for exploring new

perceptions and ways of doing things in pursuit of new truths that work for you – the teacher-artist. And in science too we hold to the notion of provisional truths, pending the rebuttal of established theory and the realisation of evidence for new hypotheses that you, the teacher-scientist, can continue to test, develop and improve.

As you are beginning to read *this* book we assume that you are interested in becoming an *inspirational* teacher, the kind of teacher that learners will remember. An inspirational teacher is one who captures a learner's imagination, challenging and moving that learner beyond 'schooling' and 'attainment' to enjoy a rich and lifelong engagement with learning. The inspirational teacher models enthusiasm for the subject and shows care for learners but is also able to hold back and take risks in allowing learners to find their own way of becoming and being (Barnett, 2007). Your memories of such a teacher will probably be from your own school or college experience. Now that you are a teacher your perspective could be very different, so you should seek out, observe and talk to the great teachers in your current workplace. Try to gain some insight into the journey they have made to become the teachers they are today, and consider what route you in turn will take.

When you watch an expert at work you may feel daunted and think, 'I will never be able to be like that.' Because teaching is largely about relationships with learners it is a very personalised and varied professional practice. You should certainly seek to learn from the expert you are observing, but you need then to work towards becoming your own style of inspirational teacher. While observing the expert we would encourage you to consider to what extent their practice is based on instinct and on practical ways of working, and to what extent it is research-informed and based on the literature on how to teach and how children and young people learn. To what extent does the lesson conform to national or institutional expectations, to the requirements of school inspectors and of the headteacher?

As with all relationships, becoming and being a teacher is not simply about developing a set of skills or techniques. Learning teaching is an emotional experience, and success will require you to strengthen a range of dispositions including your self-belief, self-awareness and resilience. In fact, the journey of becoming a teacher will be helped by you developing the same kinds of thinking dispositions that you will wish to nurture in your learners. More on that later.

You might be thinking that you need to learn to teach in the ways that are expected by school inspectors and your headteacher. There's a degree of truth in that! However, in England, for example, after 25 years of centrally controlled, detailed policy on how to teach, things are not as clear-cut as you might think. Inspectors are usually looking for engaged, focused learning and for evidence that learners are making progress. In the best cases they would hope to see that learners are being inspired by the teacher. One of the joys of teaching is that there is no global agreement on what great teaching actually is, and so becoming an inspirational teacher is a lifelong experiment in learning. We do perhaps recognise great teaching and learning when we see it, when there is challenge, trust, collaboration, enjoyment, engagement and progress in the classroom. But it is too complex, too situated in particular settings, too dependent on the identity and personality of the teacher and learners for us to be able simply to tell you how to do it. Policy-makers and politicians may strut and fret their hour upon the stage, sometimes basing their views of 'best practice' largely on their own experiences of schooling, but as a professional you must learn to question, evaluate and test policy, theory, professional guidance and research evidence, while keeping your eye firmly on the needs of your learners.

Many school systems around the world are in a period of high accountability. In England this is characterised by a national curriculum, targets based on test results, high-stakes 'name and shame' inspection processes and a competition-driven 'choice' of schools offer to parents. These kinds of school education systems appear to be truly within the 'age of measurement' (Biesta, 2011). Within this environment many schools and teachers continue to thrive and have learned to dance to the piper's tune, by teaching inspector-pleasing lessons when required and by refining their approach to maximise test results. Despite this context, many schools and teachers have managed to maintain a values-based approach and a moral purpose in their work by mediating the high-accountability external policy environment to protect their learners from its most damaging influences. This latter approach requires bold school leaders and brave teachers who may adopt an 'activist' stance (Sachs, 2003) and are willing to question policy and the wider purposes of education. In this book we offer a metaphor for teacher professional learning as **interplay** between the practical wisdom of teachers on the one hand and public (published) knowledge on the other. Many new teachers favour practical wisdom ways of working in their current school setting. While this is perfectly understandable, in this book we propose an inquiry-based approach promoting interplay between that local situated knowledge of teachers and public, published, knowledge, including learning theory, research evidence, professional guidance and policy.

Gert Biesta argues that 'education needs to have an orientation toward the freedom and independence of those being educated' (2011, p 2). From a philosophical perspective he proposes a mix of three broad purposes for education:

* qualification;
* socialisation;
* subjectification.

By **qualification** he means knowledge and certification. By **socialisation** he includes preparation for family life, citizenship and employability in a developing and uncertain world. In arguing for '**subjectification**' as an essential third purpose of education, Biesta (2011) offers a concept upon which schools and teachers may be able build their resistance to the accountability agenda and more positively drive forward their moral mission. Subjectification, as a purpose for education, means allowing children and young people the opportunity to develop as unique individuals and 'singular beings', to respond creatively to planned learning activities and occasionally to surprise their teachers.

The age of measurement does not tend to encourage such open-ended learning and prefers predictable lessons beginning and ending with reference to tightly defined intended learning outcomes. Allowing for subjectification requires schools and teachers to take risks, perhaps to 'dare' to include at least one open-ended intended learning outcome in each lesson, and to facilitate learning activities that are adventurous – meaning that the outcome is uncertain (Mortlock, 1987). In developing an education that allows subjectification, the mantra 'no risk, no learning' is a useful one. We agree with Biesta's idea that teachers must be more than competent; they must be educationally wise and have the 'ability to make situated judgements about what is educationally desirable' (Biesta, 2013).

In your engagement with this book we would encourage you to maintain a broad, values-based approach to your work and development as a teacher. We recommend that you adopt an activist stance that engages with and questions the wider purposes of education, and is aware of the contextual pressures within our age of measurement. Be brave and challenge the system! When you are more established as a professional teacher you will be able to push back against some of the flaws in the education system in which you are working, and throughout your career you will come across many teachers in schools who maintain a critical and proactive stance. In the early part of your career you might strive at least to maintain a questioning approach despite the pressures you may feel to conform, to avoid questioning current practice, to keep your head down and simply to get through your programme or probation. Position yourself heroically, as part of the solution rather than the problem. As *The Clash* put it, habituation to the prevailing order carries a risk to your own integrity:

> *You grow up and you calm down…*
>
> *you start wearing blue and brown…*
>
> *you're working for the clampdown.*

So throughout your career we ask you to maintain a questioning approach, to reject the notion that currently accepted 'best practice' is something set in stone and good for all time, to aim to contribute to progress in education rather than mere survival and the status quo. In short, we ask you to be not merely an effective teacher, but an inspirational one.

About this book

Features of this book

This book is deliberately structured to acknowledge the complexity of teaching and to provoke interplay between practical wisdom and public knowledge. There are five distinctive features.

- Each of the five 'core' chapters begins with a classroom 'scenario' involving a new teacher. This provides a grounded case study as a focus for the chapter.

- Each of the five core chapters is based on a pedagogical dilemma that teachers commonly face in their everyday work. These dilemmas acknowledge the complex orchestration that teaching involves and the choices, based on professional judgement, that you will need to make. As stated previously, we recommend that you read this book in conjunction with a more standard 'how to teach' text covering prosaic but important areas of work such as planning, inclusion, teaching, behaviour management, assessment and professional learning.

- Each of the five core chapters includes a section on 'learning power' which introduces current thinking on teaching and learning.

- Each of the five core chapters includes a section on 'workplace learning' which introduces current thinking on your professional learning as a teacher.

- The book includes regular prompts for 'things to try' and we strongly recommend that you engage with the book over a sustained period of time, interwoven with experimentation and practical changes in your classroom practice.

- By naming the five core chapters with pedagogical dilemmas we are being deliberately provocative. These dilemmas provide a useful perspective on the complex work of a teacher. As William Blake observes: 'Without contraries, there is no progression'. The dilemmas are reflected in the titles:

  - Belief versus ability;

  - Autonomy versus compliance;

  - Abstract versus concrete;

  - Feedback versus praise;

  - Collaboration versus competition.

At face value some of these dilemmas may seem confusing or even plain wrong. No problem – read on!

Dilemmas faced by teachers

Belief versus ability: Let's face it, some children are brighter than others. Not everyone can become a Professor of Astrophysics. And yet this book argues that having a growth mindset, believing that effort and deep practice will make you smarter, is more important than inherited abilities. What a dilemma for a teacher!

Autonomy versus compliance: All teachers know that well-behaved children who settle down quickly to work and do as they are told are a pleasure to have in a classroom. And yet this book emphasises the need to develop self-regulated learners who ask critical questions, think creatively and self-assess their own work. What a dilemma for a teacher!

Abstract versus concrete: Surely it is obvious that clear explanations illustrated by well-chosen, concrete examples are the bread and butter of good teaching? Authentic, practical tasks, relevant to the cultural and social lives of learners, are certainly important. And yet this book argues that teachers need to plan their key questions and learning activities around the more abstract key concepts underpinning a lesson and that meta-learning and metacognition are at least as valuable as focusing on more concrete content. What a dilemma for a teacher!

Feedback versus praise: Receiving praise is clearly motivating. Praise helps to create a positive learning environment in the classroom and school. And yet this book argues that praise – especially lavish praise – carries hidden and serious costs. Learning is enhanced by struggle, making mistakes and failing, provided that the learner receives feedback in relation to their effort, strategies and dispositions and that self-assessment is encouraged. So to praise or to offer feedback – what a dilemma for a teacher!

Collaboration versus competition: There is nothing like a bit of competition to motivate learners. It can be managed in a positive way and does not do much harm. We know that ability grouping makes teaching more manageable. And yet this book argues that working together in mixed groups is more powerful for learning. What a dilemma for a teacher!

These dilemmas reflect key issues arising from our interpretation of the educational research evidence base and our own teaching experiences. In the next sections of this introductory chapter, we will consider some basic ideas about learning. In line with the rest of the book this includes a focus first on your learners and then on your workplace learning as a teacher.

Overview of this book

Table 1.1 An overview of the core chapters (2 to 6) of this book

Chapter title: teacher's dilemma	New teacher scenario: practical wisdom	Learning power: public knowledge	Teacher workplace learning: public knowledge	Reflection on the lesson: interplay between practical wisdom and public knowledge
Chapter 2 Belief versus ability	Amy's poetry lesson: Becoming a writer	The learning power of mindset	Workplace learning: Developing teacher identity	In each core chapter we will ask you to reflect critically on the scenario before offering our own perspective. The complexity of teaching means there are no definitive answers.
Chapter 3 Autonomy versus compliance	Humza's mathematics lesson: Becoming a mathematician	The learning power of self-determination	Workplace learning: Being an inquiry-based teacher	
Chapter 4 Abstract versus concrete	David's geography lesson: Becoming a geographer	The learning power of going 'meta'	Workplace learning: Teachers' pedagogical content knowledge	

Chapter 5 Feedback versus praise	Helen's parents' evening: Becoming a self-regulated learner	The learning power of self-regulation	Workplace learning: The teacher as practitioner researcher	
Chapter 6 Collaboration versus competition	Sammie's science lesson: Becoming a scientist	The learning power of working together	Workplace learning: Teacher learning communities	

Learning power: what do we mean by 'learning'?

O this learning, what a thing it is!

(Shakespeare, *The Taming of the Shrew*,
Act 1, Scene 2, line 159)

We put the word 'learning' at the beginning of this book's title, and at the heart of every page within it. In this way we are signalling its importance and placing it alongside 'teaching' with equal weighting. We are committed to the idea that learning is for teachers as well as for their learners. Ongoing professional learning is part of becoming and being a teacher. Given its prominence in our thinking, it's worth reflecting on what exactly we mean by the word 'learning'. Most dictionary definitions of 'learning' see this concept presented quite traditionally, as *the acquisition of knowledge or skills through experience, practice or 'being taught'*. After all, it is certainly very reasonable to propose that schooling should equip learners with worthwhile cultural knowledge. This tends to be the vision of learning that is favoured by politicians and civil servants, for it is they who assume overall responsibility for ensuring that the nation's children and young people develop the skills and knowledge necessary to thrive in society. Seen through this lens, it's your job, as a teacher, to deliver these outcomes to your learners!

This vision is so familiar it is often seen as unproblematic and incontestable. So the thinking goes, 'Of course learning must involve acquiring knowledge and skills, and effective learning involves acquiring these efficiently.' Take a moment, however, to reflect on the hidden assumptions underlying this definition: the notion of 'acquiring' something implies some degree of transaction – and the necessary separation of 'that which is known' from 'the knower'. Within this conceptualisation, it's the teacher's job to find ways of efficiently transmitting the fully formed and pre-existent piece of knowledge or skill to the learner.

The view of learning as 'transmission' was well expressed some years back, in a radio exchange between the interviewer John Humphrys and the first chief inspector of English schools, Chris Woodhead (*On the Ropes*, BBC Radio 4, 29 June 2004). Woodhead was asked,

'What, for you, is the purpose of education?' The response was immediate: 'The transmission of worthwhile knowledge.' Humphrys pressed further – 'Is that all?' Slight pause, then, 'Yup, pretty much.'

If learning is merely a transaction, then Woodhead's is correct – there is not much more to education than transmission. Challenge, complexity and creativity certainly aren't players. On the contrary, there is value in keeping things simple, in ensuring that the learner 'receives' that which is 'sent' as efficiently and as speedily as possible. Challenge complicates things unnecessarily, slows down the learning-by-acquisition process and has the potential for giving rise to 'mis-deliveries' – moments where learners stray down new, unintended and probably mistaken delivery routes.

We are mindful in this book that new teachers in many countries are entering a profession in which the dominant forces at play in their training and their practice tend to go along with this traditional vision of learning: learning = being taught. So it follows naturally that learning to teach = being taught to teach – and it's the job of the people teaching the teachers to keep things simple, rapid and efficient. This is the world of pre-established and standardised 'learning outcomes' driving every lesson to pre-established outcomes, and the logical conclusion to this vision of learning and learners is 'scripted lessons'. Like learning, teaching comes down to the acquisition of certain approved skills, techniques and 'worthwhile' knowledge. It's a technical and relatively straightforward process. Do what's always been done and KISS – Keep it Simple, Stupid.

However, there is another, more ambitious, more evidence-based but also more challenging conceptualisation of learning which underpins this book and our beliefs as educators. Learning could also be seen as the *co-construction* of knowledge, skills, values and dispositions through experience, practice or 'being taught'. This implies a much more active role on the part of the learner, and a complex and multi-directional interplay between the learner, that which is learned (the curriculum) and the learning environment. It also implies that the relationship between you the teacher and your learners is not one of simply 'giving' them knowledge. The relationship between teacher and learner in this perspective is more like that of collaborators who are exploring the curriculum subject discipline together. As the teacher you are a guide or mentor, providing expert guidance and suitable inquiry-based activities to challenge the learner and help her to become a member of the subject discipline community – for example, a mathematician, a historian or a scientist. The key features of learning through construction include identification of initial ideas, leading on to exploration of possible explanations. With time to think and working within a social situation, the learner constructs new explanations.

Metaphors – linguistic representations – are helpful devices that we use to capture the human experience of learning (Lakoff and Johnson, 1980). However, dominant metaphors may be misleading (Hager, 2008). As teachers, the metaphors we hold for learning are important because they shape our conception of knowledge and our approach to teaching. The terms 'transmission' and 'construction' may be seen as contrasting metaphors for learning and each may be linked to bodies of learning theory (behaviourist and constructivist). Metaphors for learning are found in the everyday talk of teachers and their learners and are a useful way to link the everyday practical wisdom of teachers to more formal public knowledge such as learning theory.

How do these metaphors for learning play out in your actual classroom? To make the distinction between them clearer, think of some item of knowledge, concept or skill that you'd like your learners to acquire. Now imagine teaching this via transmission, and then via construction – how would these lessons be different? Table 1.2 provides a worked example.

Table 1.2 An example learning activity considered through the metaphors for learning of transmission and construction

Area of learning	Transmission	Construction
The effects of inertia	Set up an experiment where you place a small ball on a piece of paper, then pull the paper forward quickly (or more bravely, try the old pulling-the-tablecloth-from-a-set-table trick!). Point out that the ball's behaviour is explained by inertia – the tendency for a stationary object to remain stationary unless other forces act on it. Correct misconceptions, clarify the effect of friction, the need to observe the ball in relation to the wider environment – not just its position on the paper, etc. Ensure that all learners meet the desired learning outcome.	After initial modelling of the same experiment, invite your learners to work in small groups or pairs and to try out the experiment themselves and to provide three or more possible explanations for the ball's behaviour. For each explanation, seek to provide a counter-explanation. What are the conditions that affect the ball's behaviour? Ask each pair to compare their findings with another pair. Facilitate a whole-class discussion, playing devil's advocate, introducing terminology, probing for understanding, implications, consequences, etc.
Desired outcome	For learners to learn that the ball's behaviour is *explained* by the phenomenon of inertia.	For learners to learn that the ball's behaviour is *described* by the phenomenon of inertia.

This second conceptualisation of learning has a strong theoretical pedigree in the work of such twentieth-century educational giants as Vygotsky, Dewey, Piaget and Bruner. Despite this hefty theoretical hinterland, or perhaps because of it, it can be viewed with some suspicion by many politicians, press columnists, practitioners and even researchers as a relic of a former 'progressive' era. There has been considerable resistance to making a shift from considering teaching as transmission towards considering learning as construction. In part, this resistance is linked to the increasing levels of accountability in education that are based on measurement of achievement using test results – it is easier to measure learning within the 'transmission' metaphor for learning. Moreover, 'theory' seems less immediately functional: theorists haven't always been very good at making the links between theory and day-to-day real-world practice: When faced with 9Z on Friday afternoon, it's trench-lore and experience that matters, not some theoretical mumbo-jumbo! Little wonder that we often fail to see the truth of Kurt Lewin's words, that 'There's nothing more practical than a good theory' (1952, p 169). The practical wisdom of everyday practice in school is underpinned by interpretations of learning theory. When a theory is incorporated into practice it becomes 'common sense'.

Researchers who adopt a positivist perspective, such as the psychometrician John Hattie, could see educational constructivism as necessarily implying woolly, learner-led and teacher-lite approaches, rather than embodying the intense rigour that should underpin all constructivist practice. This is because constructivist practices aren't always easy to operationalise in research terms: almost by definition, constructivist approaches don't lend themselves well to tightly controlled empirical studies – there are too many complex variables at play. And richly nuanced qualitative studies on classroom learning don't compute in vast meta-study syntheses of the research evidence base. In later chapters, however, we will seek to show that the most powerful influences on learner achievement as identified by researchers like Hattie are all strongly dependent on teachers using outstanding constructivist practices.

It's worth noting here that the constructivist's synergistic interplay between teacher and learner is beautifully captured by Hattie himself in his influential book, *Visible Learning* (2009). 'Visible learning', for Hattie, is what happens when the teacher sees learning through the eyes of the learner, and the learner becomes her own teacher. Hattie believes this is what we should be aiming for as teachers, as it characterises the most powerful influences on achievement. We contend that visible learning is most likely to be found in high-quality constructivist exchanges, and will be least in evidence in those learning encounters which are essentially transactional in nature, from teacher to learner. It is ironic, therefore, that Hattie himself is sceptical about constructivism – perhaps because what has sometimes passed for 'constructivist teaching' has been undeniably weak – overvaluing learners' licence to 'explore their own learning' with minimal support and structure from the teacher. We see these instances as examples of poor teaching, not as exemplars of constructivism at work.

It is this second way of understanding learning – ie constructivism – that points us in the direction of *challenge* as a vital constituent of an outstanding education for your learners. For if learning is a dynamic, light-footed dance between multiple actors engaged in the task of knowledge or skill construction, then challenge, doubt and complexity are to be valued and pursued as fertile territory for the construction of both deep *and* surface meanings, for the asking of new questions and the exploration of new lines of inquiry. Because teaching, like medicine, law and any advanced profession, is *not* an exact science: 'Uncertainty is the parent of professionalism and the enemy of standardisation' (Hargreaves and Fullan, 2012, p 107). Or as Lawrence Stenhouse put it, 'Education as induction into knowledge is successful to the extent that it makes the behavioural outcomes of the students unpredictable' (Stenhouse, 1975, p 82). This links to the idea developed by Gert Biesta (2013) that the complexity of teaching and the multiple paradigms and ways of knowing within the field of education make it necessary to trust teachers' professional judgements and accept the 'beautiful' risk of education.

In the past, when we undertook our own postgraduate teacher education programmes, it was impressed on us that we must differentiate the work we set our learners. What we took this to mean was that the work we set our learners should be 'pitched to their ability'. If we did our job well, then any one learner should receive work that she could do – and without too much of a struggle. In practice, this meant that we spent time dooming our learners to relatively easy successes and making them vulnerable to the infrequent experience of struggle, setbacks and 'failures'. This is the fast-track to developing passive, unresourceful learners who show as much stickability as a Teflon-coated pan. When challenge is a consistent and well-measured part of their everyday classroom diet, however, learners learn to reach further and deeper in their learning, and to build the reservoirs of resilience, grit and intrinsic interest that will sustain them in all learning encounters. It is helpful to reflect on examples such as learning to ride a bike or to drive a car. These usually involve another and more skilled person (a teacher), require both learner and teacher to take risks and require persistence. Both of these considerable challenges, for most people, are about mastery; failure is only temporary and persistence and practice at the edge of current skill levels will eventually lead to success.

We would like to give you a contrasting message about differentiation from the outset: differentiation is important, but see this as differentiation by challenge – not ability (ability is an alluring but dead-end concept educationally speaking – see the next chapter). Ask yourself: 'Is this work likely to challenge this learner?' If it is, then great, just make sure that it isn't way too much of a challenge – or at the very least make sure that the high challenge is matched by the high quality of feedback the learner receives. If it isn't sufficiently challenging, then up the ante, and fast! Challenge is a relative concept – relative to a learner's current levels of achievement. When differentiating by challenge (not ability), aim ultimately for a roughly 50:50 ratio of success to failure. 'Is this work likely to present this learner with a roughly 50 per cent prospect of success, or is it more like 90 per cent?' When there's a significant prospect of failure the expectation builds in the learner that learning is necessarily hard work – otherwise, it's simply practising past learning! Learners must stop seeing 'failure' as something to avoid, as the source of humiliation, but as evidence that new learning is struggling effortfully into existence. The 50:50 ratio is of course a rule of thumb only, and you'll need to be flexible with some learners as you wean them off an expectation of initial success.

The entrepreneur and *Dragons' Den* star Peter Jones said in an interview, 'There's a word that resonates in schools and that's "failure": you pass or fail', says Jones. 'But what enterprise and entrepreneurship does is show that there is no such thing as failure, there's only feedback. I think that's a really important message to tell every child' (Peter Jones, *Telegraph*, 16 March 2015).

However noble, true and aspirational the second conceptualisation of learning as 'construction' and its implications for challenge might seem, is it any good to you as a teacher? Is it compatible with your own early experiences? Is it compatible with an assessment system that seems bounded by 'right answers' and a settled curriculum? Is it compatible with the organisational structures within which you work? Will it be tolerated by your senior leaders, mentors and the inspection system they must respond to? Let's be quite clear from the start about our position on all these questions:

1. Only you, through a process of active and honest reflection, will be able to gauge the extent to which each understanding of 'learning' matches your own experiences in the classroom. This book will act as a guide to these reflections. Will you see your learners acquiring pre-existent knowledge via efficient and predictable transactions, or will you instead witness what at times seems to be – even (perhaps especially) in well-managed and task-focused classrooms – a whirring confusion of influences and outcomes?

2. Though you might in fact reach your peak as a teacher only after about eight years in the job (Day and Gu, 2010), new teachers have the right to be outstanding from an early stage in their careers, and your response to challenges and your purposeful creation of challenges for your learners will be an important part of making this happen. The notion of challenge is one we return to throughout this book, and we ask that you value it in all its manifestations.

3. There is no contradiction between the challenge of constructivism with its emphasis on the active roles of both teacher *and* learner and the demands of the assessment system. On the contrary, there is a strong link between the two. In most classrooms pursuing the traditional view of learning, teachers take the lead in setting targets and challenges for their learners. But when learners are tasked with setting their own challenges and goals, some astonishing effects can be seen. In fact, some research has found that the academic performances of learners with the most challenging goals are 250 per cent (!) higher than those with the easiest goals (Wood and Locke, 1987). And John Hattie, in his huge and ongoing synthesis of multiple studies, makes it clear just why challenge is so important in promoting learning and achievement: 'Challenges help to make learning easier and thereby have positive effects on long-term retention' (Hattie, 2012, p 102). Counter-intuitive but true!

4. School inspectors are generally explicit about the value they place on challenge. In fact, if your lesson is consistently low on challenge, then you can kiss goodbye to any hopes of great performance data and achieving a top grade from a classroom observer.

In Chapter 2 we unpick all of this in more detail, when we concentrate on the role of *mindset* in your development as a teacher and your learners' development as learners.

Things to try

» *Think of a key concept, big idea or skill that you would like your learners to engage with, and as shown in Table 1.2 try to sketch out a design for a learning activity or lesson from a perspective of learning as 'transmission' and as 'construction'.*

» *Observe a lesson taught by a colleague or make a video of one of your own lessons. Evaluate the lesson in terms of the metaphors for learning as 'transmission' and as 'construction'. Consider if the lesson might be redesigned to be stronger in terms of learning as construction.*

> »   *Ask yourself if there are any situational nudges you might experience when planning to teach for transmission or for co-construction. For instance, is one approach more likely to be tried when you're working with a lower- or upper-set group? With an older or younger class? With a more or less socially skilled group?*

Teachers: professional learning as 'interplay'

This section focuses on your professional learning as a teacher. In this book we offer a new situated metaphor for teacher learning as **interplay** between the horizontal domain of practical wisdom and the vertical domain of public knowledge.

As we have already seen, metaphors are powerful ways to capture the essence of learning and we all use them frequently to understand our practice as teachers. A metaphor for learning is a figure of speech that identifies learning as being the same as some other unrelated activity. So if we suggest 'giving' you some information or 'delivering' a lesson, then we are using a transmission metaphor for learning. It is helpful to link such metaphors to different theories of learning.

We might suggest that the next section of this book will 'give' you some information or knowledge, as if knowledge might be like a nicely wrapped present. You may think that you can collect such fragments of knowledge and build them into a pile or body of knowledge. These kinds of metaphorical statements refer to the most widely used 'transmission' or 'acquisition' metaphors for learning and may be aligned with a behaviourist theory of learning as transmission.

Alternatively, we might work on a problem together and reach a shared understanding through dialogue around an issue or perhaps eventually agree to differ about the best solution. The learning involved might best be expressed as 'participation' or 'construction', which is a metaphor that is more aligned to social constructivist learning theory and is widely used by teachers and teacher educators as a rationale for active and collaborative learning strategies.

In a study of teachers in Spain the majority of metaphors for learning (technically these were similes because they compare using terms such as 'like' or 'as') were related to transmission, such as 'learning is like a sponge which soaks in the water'. Another large group of similes held by the teachers were constructivist, such as 'learning is like setting the bricks of a house. The learner is the mason and the house at the same time. S/he is also the owner of the house. The teacher is the site foreman.' Only two (5 per cent) of the similes offered by the teachers in the study were more closely related to situated or workplace learning theory; one referred to ants working together and the other used the idea of a tour guide negotiating an itinerary with their group of tourists for a visit to an unknown place (Martinez et al, 2001).

This third group of metaphors, including 'contribution' or 'becoming', have developed through study of workplace learning and may be linked to situated learning theory (Lave and Wenger, 1991; Wenger, 1998). These metaphors acknowledge the mediated, situated, social, dynamic and contested nature of professional knowing (Blackler, 1995). Metaphors for professional learning as 'becoming' also take account of the identity building involved, for example, as you 'become' a teacher (Wenger, 1998; Hager, 2008). Situated learning theory highlights a key challenge as you become a teacher: you need to learn through working in particular schools but you are preparing for a career in which you will need to be able to work in a variety of settings and contribute to wider networks. Local ways of working among teachers in your placement or first school post will be a powerful influence on you. You are likely to learn a great deal from local ways of learning, but this practical wisdom, 'what works here', must not overwhelm your ability to question what you see and do, and you should actively seek external perspectives by engagement with the literature as well as with external colleagues and networks.

The professional development of teachers sometimes suffers from a dominant but misleading metaphor of the 'gap' between theory and practice. This metaphor is frequently used by teacher educators and is often taken for granted in research and professional guidance publications. The problem with the 'gap' metaphor is that it assumes a separation between 'theory' and 'practice' as if these were two distinct bodies of knowledge. This misleading way of considering professional knowledge has developed in a higher education context where traditional subject disciplines have dominated and professional fields such as teacher or nurse education may be considered as peripheral newcomers.

This book explicitly adopts and builds on an alternative metaphor for teachers' professional learning as 'interplay' between the vertical domain of public knowledge (theory, research, professional guidance and policy) and the horizontal domain of teachers' practical wisdom – local ways of working within specific school settings (Boyd, 2014; Boyd and Bloxham, 2014). In this metaphor for teachers' learning, the vertical and horizontal domains of knowledge are seen as interconnected dimensions rather than distinct bodies of knowledge. The 'interplay' metaphorical framework is illustrated in Figure 1.1.

The complexity of teacher knowing does not allow a simplistic distinction between public knowledge and practical wisdom. By this we mean that within the practice of a teacher or team of teachers there will be elements of public (published) knowledge but its interpretation and application through a complex social process may make it appear as a simple routine or way of working. For example, in a typical school the teachers' everyday approach to engaging learners and managing their behaviour will often reflect research-based findings often referred to as the 'behaviour for learning' literature. The teachers concerned, however, may sometimes be unaware of the link to public knowledge, or in some cases may even vehemently deny that their practice is research-informed!

The horizontal domain of teachers' practical wisdom foregrounds the practical ways of working that are dominant within a particular school setting. This knowledge is held socially by the team of teachers and teaching assistants and will include unwritten rules and 'tacit' knowledge (hard to explain or write down). Buried within this practical wisdom will be hidden the mediated bones of public knowledge. The teachers have adapted theory, professional guidance and policy to their way of working and the features of their particular setting. Using the term 'practical wisdom' for this domain of teacher knowledge is a deliberate attempt to acknowledge the significance of classroom teacher expertise that is based on doing the job at the 'chalkface'. This domain of knowledge is horizontal because it changes from one setting to another and is developed and held by teams of teachers collaborating with their peers.

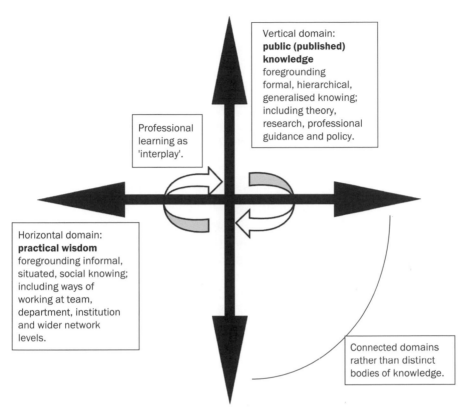

Figure 1.1 *Teacher professional learning as 'interplay' between practical wisdom and public knowledge (Boyd, 2014; Boyd and Bloxham, 2014)*

The vertical domain of public knowledge consists of published literature including learning theory, research papers, professional guidance texts and official policy. This domain of knowledge is vertical because it is hierarchically ordered through the processes of peer review and publication. This publication process creates and reflects power within the vertical knowledge domain. For example, a text gains status through its publication by a well-established educational publisher, or through online peer review. A paper gains status through publication in a peer-reviewed research journal and through citation by other writers. National government policy also has high status and even a local school policy gains an element of power through publication. However, despite the more abstract and generalised nature of this vertical knowledge it cannot be separated completely from more mundane and common-sense judgements. The best theoretical writing will use concrete examples and practitioners at least will partly understand theory through their application of the idea to their own work context or experience.

The vertical and horizontal domains of knowledge are therefore not distinct bodies of knowledge but rather form two dimensions of teacher knowing.

Interplay

Within this metaphorical framework, the term 'interplay' is intended to capture the power and tension involved in teacher learning within the relationships between teachers, school leaders, inspectors and teacher educators (Boyd, 2014; Boyd and Bloxham, 2014). However, 'interplay' is also intended to capture the fun and creativity involved in working with children and young people to plan, teach and evaluate learning outcomes. From a sociocultural or situated learning perspective, the term 'interplay' helps to capture the 'dynamic' and 'contested' characteristics of professional knowledge, which is better expressed as professional 'knowing' (Blackler, 1995). This metaphor of interplay also helps to acknowledge the role of artefacts in teacher learning. These artefacts may be practical objects such as a school policy or scheme of work, but they may also include abstract concepts used in your workplace such as 'excellent work' or 'critical thinking'.

The interplay metaphor arises from a third area of learning theory, alongside behaviourism and constructivism, which strongly influences the view of teachers' workplace learning adopted in this book. This third perspective is known as 'situated learning theory' and was strongly influenced by the work of Lave and Wenger who studied apprenticeships in a range of different contexts (Lave and Wenger, 1991; Wenger, 1998). Lave and Wenger developed the concept of the 'legitimate peripheral participation' of a newcomer in a workplace, as they learn the written and unwritten rules and through negotiation gradually earn membership of the 'community of practice'. Situated learning theory provides a useful perspective through which to consider the agency of the teacher, their power and influence as an individual, within their workplace context. As a new teacher you may feel that you do not wield much power, but in fact in your classroom you are the expert and have considerable autonomy and influence over the experiences of your learners. Developing your expertise and confidence will enable you increasingly to take charge and to contribute to development in and beyond your own classroom. That is what becoming a professional teacher is about and this book aims to support you in that journey.

By adopting the metaphor of teacher learning through 'interplay' as the basis for this book, we will strive to maintain a balance between the research evidence base and the situated knowledge of teachers. For example, the sections of each chapter on 'learning power' are greatly informed by meta-reviews of research and in particular by John Hattie's work on visible learning. In referring throughout this book to John Hattie's work, and other work based on research meta-review, we will be using the technical term 'effect size'. Research meta-reviews involve systematic selection of research studies and a collation of the evidence they provide. Effect size is a way of capturing the impact of an intervention and expresses the change in achievement of an 'experimental' group over a control group. So, for example, if one mathematics class experienced formative assessment intervention and the control class did not, then the difference in results of a standardised mathematics test could be used to calculate the effect size. An effect size of d = 0.8 means that the score of an average person in the experimental class is higher than 79 per cent of students in the control class as seen in Figure 1.2. It is possible to have a negative effect size, in which case the intervention is slowing the learning progress of the class. Hattie makes a reasonable argument that effect sizes of 0.4 or more are worthy of serious attention by educators and policy-makers (2012, p 14). For a lucid introduction to the nature and application of effect sizes, have a look at Robert Coe's explanation in www.leeds.ac.uk/educol/documents/00002182.htm. However, it is important to acknowledge the limitations of research meta-reviews, in particular, their selection of research studies that allow calculation of effect size (but which might nonetheless offer rich and nuanced

Effect Size	% of the control group who would be below the average person in the experimental (intervention) group
0.0	50
0.2	58
0.4	66
0.6	73
0.8	79
1.0	86
1.4	92
1.8	96
2.0	98
3.0	99.9

Figure 1.2 *A statistical interpretation of 'effect size'*

information about the effects of an intervention). While we value their powerful contribution to developing research-informed practice, and have taken on board the key messages of research reviews, we also value a wide range of approaches to educational research and in particular believe that mixed-methods studies and practitioner research, by and with teachers, make a critical contribution to knowledge creation and the development of effective practice.

Things to try

» Reflect on, and try to write down, some of the key features of good teaching that represent the practical wisdom of teachers in your school. What kind of teaching is highly valued? What are the characteristics of teaching practice that are seen as excellent or 'best practice'?

» Consider to what extent teaching in your school appears to be 'research-informed', meaning that practice is based to some extent on public knowledge in the form of learning theory, research evidence or professional guidance texts. To what extent is critical engagement with public knowledge valued and seen as part of the normal work of teachers and school leaders?

Using this book

Newly armed with metaphors for learning as transmission and construction and for teachers' professional learning as interplay, it is time to launch into the core chapters of this book.

There are five core chapters in this book and you might consider reading through them in a linear fashion. To some extent we have assumed this rather conventional approach and so we make some assumptions in later sections that you have already read through and reflected on the previous chapters. However, this book is not intended to be a simple matter of reading from start to finish, because if it is to achieve its aims then we need you to return to this book having tried to implement some of its ideas within your classroom teaching.

Each of the five core chapters is therefore to some extent designed as a stand-alone resource. You might be interested in developing a 'growth mindset' (Dweck, 2006) in yourself as a teacher or in your learners. In this case it would be worth engaging with and returning to Chapter 2. If you feel a focus on developing your learners or yourself as questioning critical thinkers is important, then Chapter 3 is worth a visit. However, if you are focusing on learning within a curriculum subject and are considering the planning of learning activities, then Chapter 4 deserves your particular attention. For a focus on assessment and feedback, Chapter 5 will be useful. If group work and collaborative learning are on your agenda, then Chapter 6 is your next port of call.

As a teacher you will have some concern for the formal assessment of your practice and the professional judgements that colleagues and headteachers may make about your teaching. You will be partly focused on professional standards for teachers and on the official curriculum in your institutional and national context. You will also be keenly aware of quality assurance processes within your setting, including internal and external school inspection regimes and processes. This book is designed to help you develop as a teacher, but we focus unapologetically on learning and ask you to complete the task of mapping across to your particular policy framework and school context.

However you decide to work with this book, try not to rush through, unless you intend to return to it more slowly at a later date. In particular, we would encourage you to engage with the reflective tasks we have proposed and to interrupt your reading with practical activity in your classroom. Based on your reading you might try to make small changes in your practice and evaluate their impact. We have tried our best to keep this book concise and accessible, but each chapter covers a good deal of ground and will benefit from your full engagement, application to practice, rereading and reflective thinking.

As you experience the challenges of becoming a teacher, this book aims to provide a reassuring guide to let you know that your ambition to become a great and influential teacher is worthwhile, and to provide some key ideas and tools to support you on your journey. Capturing the imagination of young people, motivating them to a deep engagement with learning, encouraging them to embrace challenge and above all being willing to take risks so that your learners are able to find their own way of becoming and being – these ambitions have no easy tick list of technical solutions. They provide a worthy challenge for you in your developing career as an inspirational teacher.

Chapter 1 summary

This first chapter has presented an overview of this book to prepare you for the five 'core' chapters. It has also introduced some basic learning theory in relation to your learners and to your own workplace learning.

Learning power

- Metaphors for learning are useful and 'transmission' and 'construction' helpfully link to behaviourist and constructivist theories of how children and young people learn.

- High-quality constructivist learning is captured by Hattie's idea of 'visible learning', meaning that the teacher sees learning through the eyes of the learner, and the learner becomes her own teacher.

- A 50:50 ratio of success to failure in learning activities is a good rule of thumb for a classroom where expectations are high for all learners, challenge is embraced by learners, the risk of failure is seen as fun and mistakes are an opportunity for learning.

Teachers' workplace learning

- The practical wisdom of teachers in a particular school seems to be all about 'ways of working' and 'what works with our learners', but in the background it does build on foundations of learning theory, research evidence, professional guidance and policy.

- The public, published, knowledge in the field of education foregrounds learning theory, research evidence, professional guidance and policy, but it is contested. There are multiple views on any particular issue, and one way of evaluating such public knowledge is to consider its relevance to practice in a particular school or classroom.

- It is helpful to consider teachers' professional learning as 'interplay' between practical wisdom and public knowledge. This interplay involves power and working relationships and is affected by the value placed on different kinds of knowledge within your school.

Taking it further

It is important to keep an eye on the big picture. These three books are recommended reading on the purpose of education and the expertise of teachers:

Biesta, G. J. J. (2011) *Good Education in an Age of Measurement: Ethics, Politics, Democracy*. Boulder, CO: Paradigm.

A concise, accessible but thought-provoking and scholarly book that argues for radical change in schooling to embrace its wider purposes beyond passing exams and preparing to join the workforce.

Claxton, G. (2008) *What's the Point of School? Rediscovering the Heart of Education*. Oxford: OneWorld.

This accessible book provides a powerful argument for reform of schooling to focus on developing learner dispositions.

Eaude, T. (2012) *How Do Expert Primary Classteachers Really Work? A Critical Guide for Teachers, Headteachers and Teacher Educators*. Northwich: Critical Publishing.

A concise and accessible book about the expertise of good teachers and the way that they handle the complex, multiple and sometimes contradictory aims of education. It complements and extends the 'teachers' workplace learning' sections of this book.

References

Barnett, R. (2007) *A Will to Learn: Being a Student in an Age of Uncertainty*. Maidenhead: Open University Press.

Biesta, G. J. J. (2011) *Good Education in an Age of Measurement: Ethics, Politics, Democracy*. Boulder, CO: Paradigm.

Biesta, G. J. J. (2013) *The Beautiful Risk of Education*. London: Paradigm.

Blackler, F. (1995) Knowledge, Knowledge Work and Organizations: An Overview and Interpretation. *Organization Studies*, 6, pp 1021–46.

Boyd, P. (2014) Learning Teaching in School. In H. Cooper (ed.) *Professional Studies in Primary Education* (2nd edn). London: Sage, pp 267–88. Companion website available at: www.uk.sagepub.com/upm-data/61142_Cooper.pdf (accessed 1 May 2015).

Boyd, P. and Bloxham, S. (2014) A Situative Metaphor for Teacher Learning: The Case of University Tutors Learning to Grade Student Coursework. *British Educational Research Journal*, 40(2), pp 337–52.

Day, C. and Gu, Q. (2010) *The New Lives of Teachers: Teacher Quality and School Development*. Abingdon: Routledge.

Dweck, C. S. (2006) *Mindset: The New Psychology of Success*. New York: Random House.

Eisner, E. W. (1998) *The Kind of Schools We Need: Personal Essays*. Portsmouth: Heinemann.

Hager, P. (2008) Learning and Metaphors. *Medical Teacher*, 30(7), pp 679–86.

Hargreaves, A. and Fullan, M. (2012) *Professional Capital: Transforming Teaching in Every School*. Columbia, NY: Teachers College Press.

Hattie, J. (2009) *Visible Learning: A Synthesis of Over 800 Meta-Analyses Relating to Achievement*. Abingdon: Routledge.

Hattie, J. (2012) *Visible Learning for Teachers: Maximising Impact on Learning*. Abingdon: Routledge.

Lakoff, G. and Johnson, M. (1980) *Metaphors We Live By*. Chicago: Chicago University Press.

Lave, J. and Wenger, E. (1991) *Situated Learning: Legitimate Peripheral Participation*. Cambridge: Cambridge University Press.

Lewin, K. (1952) *Field Theory in Social Science: Selected Theoretical Papers*. London: Tavistock.

Martinez, M. A., Sauleda, N. and Huber, G. L. (2001) Metaphors as Blueprints of Thinking about Teaching and Learning. *Teaching and Teacher Education*, 17(8), pp 965–77.

Mortlock, C. (1987) *The Adventure Alternative*. Milnthorpe: Cicerone.

Sachs, J. (2003) *The Activist Teaching Profession*. Maidenhead: Open University Press.

Stenhouse, L. (1975) *An Introduction to Curriculum Research and Development*. London: Heinemann.

Wenger, E. (1998) *Communities of Practice: Learning, Meaning, and Identity*. Cambridge: Cambridge University Press.

Wood, R. E. and Locke, E. A. (1987) The Relation of Self-Efficacy and Grade Goals to Academic Performance. *Educational and Psychological Measurement*, 47(4), pp 1013–24.

Chapter 2 Belief versus ability

This chapter is about

*   **the nature of 'intelligence', 'ability' and 'potential';**
*   **the idea of fixed and growth mindsets;**
*   **personal teacher identity and how that identity is shaped.**

Introduction

This chapter interrogates a few central questions around teaching and learning. Your answers to these questions are likely to provide a framing architecture for your behaviour and expectations throughout your career, so it's as well to address them early and to keep returning to them: What do you understand to be the nature of intelligence? What do you think is the relationship between intelligence and achievement? How do your personal beliefs about intelligence impact on your learners?

In the course of responding to these questions we'd like you to question your responses in relation not only to your learners but also in relation to yourself. For example, is your own intelligence fixed or is it malleable? Is it inherited or is it acquired? Is it important or is it incidental? Is it defined by your 'IQ' or by much broader indicators? We will, as usual, present our own views explicitly, but we will ask you to retain a critical edge of your own, and to question whether we've made a convincing case for our arguments. We will, for instance, assert that the term 'ability' is widely used within many schools in an unintentionally damaging and demotivating way because it can imply that learners 'have' intelligence as a rather random gift (the accident of parental genes?) rather than developing it through assiduous effort and response to feedback. Also, we will sometimes seek to reconcile polarised debates in favour of more nuanced syntheses: for example, we don't argue for the *irrelevance* of concepts like intelligence, ability and talent, we argue instead that they are dangerously beset by misconceptions and represent only the starting points for ultimate achievement. As such, we believe the tired old debates of nature *versus* nurture offer little to contemporary practitioners when all the current evidence supports the inextricably interrelated aspect of nature *and* nurture – that they are inseparably bound up in each other.

From the end of the twentieth century onwards, traditional notions of 'natural ability' were giving ground to contemporary perspectives which argued persuasively that intelligence – however defined – is 'learnable' (eg Gardner, 1984; Sharron, 1994; Perkins, 1995; Sternberg, 1997), and it is this contemporary evidence that causes us to take issue with embedded practices in many schools.

From the perspective that intelligence is learnable, effort and practice at the edge of current ability will develop a brain like a muscle and make it stronger (Claxton, 2002; Dweck, 2006). A key message is that practice at the edge of your current ability promotes learning and that making mistakes and correcting for them needs to part of this practice (Ericsson, 2009). Others argue more from a social perspective that intelligence is the ability to succeed in life within your cultural context, and that this requires analytical, creative and practical components that are learnable (Sternberg, 1997). We urge you to reflect on your beliefs and assumptions about the 'potential' and 'ability' of your learners and about your own developing intelligence as you become a teacher. Your beliefs are revealed to your learners through interactions and through the expectations you hold.

The teacher dilemma 'belief versus ability' may seem to contradict your current thinking and go against the grain of traditional and still widely held views in society about intelligence, talent and personality. We argue that you need to believe that learners can become more intelligent through persistent effort on challenging tasks. We need to resist labelling learners in terms of 'ability' or 'potential' and allow them to learn without limits. Read on and consider for yourself.

CLASSROOM SCENARIO

Amy's poetry lesson

I am so pleased I have an exam class of 15-year-olds as part of my first teaching placement, but I am less pleased that the class teacher has said I need to cover poetry with them. To be completely honest with you, it's just not my strong point, though I feel a little bit uncomfortable admitting this. It was my least favourite aspect of English when I was at school myself, and I seemed to manage to avoid doing all that much of it during my degree. And now here I am, responsible for what these students are going to write in their exam. I have looked through the exam board's anthology they have to study poems from. I have read mountains of stuff about the poems that a Google search happily chucked back at me. I am lucky enough to be in a great department, they have stacks of resources and are very open about sharing them – expanding collections are growing on my computer desktop and under my actual desk. The class teacher has asked me to look at the unseen poem with them – this is a question they have to answer in the exam about a poem they have never seen before. The first thought that came into my mind was, 'Oh no, that means I can't Google it.'

The class is set 4 out of six 'ability' sets and their predicted examination grades are Ds and Es – anyone with the hope of getting the magic C grade has already been moved up to the 'borderline' set 3, so in the words of another member of the department, 'You've got your work cut out for you. They know they aren't going to get Cs, so most of them stopped caring round about the start of October.' Great. A poem no one understands for a class that doesn't care.

The class's usual teacher is extremely passionate about teaching English, and she has a great relationship with the class, but she has told me that she is finding it a challenge to get them to understand the poems they have to write about from the anthology in the time available – she has only been able to cover three of those poems so far. Her advice is to introduce them to one new poem every lesson using the anthology, and to treat that as an 'unseen' poem, so killing two birds with one stone – teaching them skills to handle an unseen poem, and ticking off some more of the poems we know they have to answer questions on. Sounds reasonable enough, and when I heard it I breathed a huge sigh of relief because at least I'd be able to research the poem myself first, knowing there would be plenty of resources about it. Also, she is under pressure to start the next topic with them after half-term, so time is tight. Time is always tight, that is one of the key things I am learning about teaching, particularly the teaching of exam classes.

So I had my first lesson with them last week. My main worry was just getting them to concentrate for the lesson, not to kick off. It's the first time I've taught this age range, and though I want the experience, it does seem like a challenge. I'd been told I had to cover the Owen Sheers poem 'Mametz Wood' from the exam board anthology. This is a poem about part of the Battle of the Somme, when 4000 men were lost reclaiming some woodland. The poem talks about how today farmers still find bones from the dead men when they dig the soil. It's a horrible thought, and the poem tells it like it is.

I decided to start getting them to spot the alliteration because there is a lot of it in the poem. I was told they had previously learned about alliteration, but surprise, surprise, a lot of them could not remember what it is, so I had to tell them, and that took up more time than I had planned. Then I had a worksheet helping them to spot the imagery because all the stuff I read about the poem said that that was really important. I'd spent a long time designing the worksheet, I put images on it and printed it out in colour, and I'd made sure I understood all the imagery myself; it is pretty powerful stuff. I was really pleased at the end of the lesson because they all had quite a lot of notes in their books, and lots of them had highlighted the imagery and alliteration. I was surprised how neatly a lot of them did this. The behaviour wasn't anywhere near as bad as I had feared. Disaster avoided, major sigh of relief. SO I'm thinking that maybe this technique of keeping them busy with short tasks is going to work well with them. I was pretty pleased with it all, to be honest; it could have been a lot worse. My first lesson with this age range, no major incidents, I gave myself a pat on the back. One of them even said something really amazing about his great-granddad being in the Battle of the Somme and he said he would bring in his medal for the next lesson. I hope we've got time to look at it, because we have to move on to another poem next lesson, and that isn't a World War I poem at all. Anyway, it is good he showed an interest.

As the class teacher was OK with what I'd done, I'm thinking now that I'll continue with this model for the rest of the poetry lessons, and so I'm hopeful that we will get through all the poems she wants me to cover. I've got all the resources, and I know what works with the class, so this isn't going to be as big a worry as I first thought.

Questions about Amy's lesson

1. Is there a sense that Amy's expectations of this class are lower because it is a low set, and the fact she has been told they will not secure a C grade? How far are her expectations borne out of the view of others in the school?

2. How far do you think Amy's aspirations for the lesson are limited by her own feelings about poetry and her ability to teach it? What is the relationship between her longstanding disenchantment with and avoidance of poetry at school and university and her perceived lack of ability to teach it?

3. To what extent can you connect with Amy's feelings about the boy who offered to bring in an ancestor's war medal – the tension between curriculum progression and honouring a learner's engagement?

4. To what extent does Amy seem open to developing her own curriculum subject knowledge around poetry? Amy says she is 'pretty pleased' with the lesson at the end. Do you think it is reasonable she should think this (she does overcome some major worries about her ability to work with this class), or should she have higher expectations for herself, and consequently for the lesson?

5. Amy is supposed to be teaching the students about the 'unseen' poetry element of the exam, but she ends up covering a poem from their anthology, and seems to forget about the initial idea for the lesson. Why do you think this is?

6. Amy is following guidance from the experienced teacher. It may be very tricky for a new teacher to go against the established ways of working in a teaching team. Do you think it is realistic for Amy to think for herself and even challenge the practical wisdom of the experienced teacher?

7. Amy's approach to the poem allows the class to have made some notes about the poem, and to identify some 'features' of the poem (alliteration and imagery), so there is some tangible evidence the students have done something. Is there any evidence the students have *learnt* something, however?

Take a few moments to reflect on your response to Amy's lesson and to the questions above. As you read through the following sections, on learning power and then on teachers' workplace learning, try to keep the scenario in mind. We will return to a discussion of Amy's lesson towards the end of the chapter. It is particularly useful if you begin to relate some of the issues raised in Amy's scenario to your own practice.

LEARNING POWER

The learning power of mindset

One of the most common misconceptions in education – and one that some teachers spend their entire careers holding – is that *ability* is the most important determinant of future educational outcomes. It makes sense superficially ('bright' learners achieve more highly – doh!), but when examined more deeply, it becomes clear that ability (or more accurately, skills) is itself acquired over time and in response to opportunity and the investment of effort – it doesn't just emerge. Graham Nuthall, who studied learning in naturalistic classroom environments for longer and in more detail than arguably any other researcher, put it beautifully: 'Ability appears to be the consequence, not the cause of differences in what learners learn from their classroom experiences' (Nuthall, 1999, p 213).

We see it as our task in this chapter to reject the misconceptions around 'ability' and to invite you instead to spend a career in teaching with these misconceptions consigned to the bin, where they belong. If you can do this, not only will you have raised expectations for all your learners – and raised performances as a result – you will also cope better with the challenges that your chosen profession will certainly put before you throughout your career. We invite you to consider the evidence that what individuals *believe* about ability (their own or anyone else's) is far more significant educationally than the ability itself.

Lifelong learning achievement

Let us start, however, by being clear about what we're *not* saying. We are not saying that all children enter your classes with identical capabilities, levels of understanding and achievement, or even potentials for understanding or achievement. We are not denying the indisputably high correlation between measures of ability (like IQ or CAT scores) and school performance outcomes. After all, these tests were designed from the outset to help predict children's school performances. And they do it rather well – albeit by no means 100 per cent accurately. And we are certainly not going to insist that all children are 'gifted'.

What we *are* saying is that no one knows what the lifelong learning achievement of any individual will be – whatever his or her baseline. We don't, you don't, the Fischer Family Trust don't and not even the individual herself knows the level or breadth she'll be performing at in six months' time – let alone in six years or more. Target and predicted grades are a rough and ready reckoner, not a window into the future. 'Potential' is an even fuzzier word than ability. Someone's 'potential' is unknown and unknowable – we can't second-guess what might be achieved with sufficient opportunity, endeavour and resilience. Resist the temptation to promise in your career to help a child 'realise her potential' (or reach it, or fulfil it, or achieve it). You will *never* know when you can claim to have done that. The most you can honestly claim is to seek to help a child to *develop* her (unknown) potential.

Within a constructivist rather than technical-rational vision of learning, future achievement is always a present unknown, affected as it is by a vast range of overlapping influences.

'Ability' as defined by psychometric test scores will be just one influence – and by no means the most important one. In the words of the old saying: hard work beats talent when talent doesn't work hard. Ability is important only in the context of motivation (really wanting something), volition (having the willpower to put the wanting into action) and opportunity. If ability alone were the sole determinant of achievement there'd be no such thing as an 'able underachiever' or the opposite – a child of modest abilities who goes on to excel through hard work, persistence and drive.

In the West, however, and at least for the last 150 years, we have had a rather touching faith in intellectual determinism – the idea that one's intelligence defines one's future – and our practices have reflected this. To the present day, most primary and secondary schools group their learners by ability some of the time – for instance, in numeracy or literacy sets. Some do this all of the time – for instance, in selective schools or in those schools that use streaming. Social policy often outstrips social science. The actual evidence for ability grouping is marginal at best, and at worst it's non-existent: Hattie's summary of the evidence makes for sober reading, whether we're looking at attainment outcomes, effects on self-concept, attitudes towards subjects or educational equity. Especially vulnerable are the members of 'bottom set' classes. Marzano et al (2001) cite an astonishingly worrying effect size of *minus* 0.6 for learners placed in low-ability classes – equivalent to a percentile *loss* of 23 (Lou et al, 1996, cited in Marzano et al, 2001). This is a remarkable effect since with very few exceptions the vast majority of educational practices have small or larger *positive* influences on learner achievement, as indeed anyone who believes that education confers value might hope! And do be aware that mixed-ability teaching is not the antidote to grouping by ability: even in schools that practise mixed-ability teaching, the emphasis is still on *ability* as the concept that fuels the furnace of classroom structures.

Despite the continued dominance of *ability* in our school system, and the overt or insidious pressures that keep it there, there are many inspirational accounts of schools and teachers that have rejected this concept in favour of more powerful and less deterministic influences on achievement. Some of these are described in the 'Learning without Limits' project which has been supported by Cambridge University for over a decade (see Hart et al, 2004; Swann et al, 2012).

Of course, these data are all very well to consider at a senior leadership level, but what can you do, as a beginning teacher, to mitigate the worst effects of setting or streaming in the classes you're given to teach? Actually, a whole range of things – explored within this book, and all deriving from or connected to the concept of *mindset* (Dweck, 2000, 2006; Hymer and Gershon, 2014).

Mindset

> *Whether you think you can, or whether you think you can't, you're right.*

> (Henry Ford)

For very many years, led by the groundbreaking work of Carol Dweck of Stanford University, researchers have found that what an individual *believes* about her ability has a profound effect on her learning behaviour. Broadly, Dweck identifies two groups of people.

Some people believe that ability is a stable trait that is largely impervious to such external influences as teaching and other learning opportunities. These people hold a *fixed mind-set*. They tend to avoid, resist or ignore a wide range of important educational opportunities for learning. These include challenges, mistakes, effort, critical feedback and others' successes. With their *fixed mindsets*, these individuals' responses are perfectly rational, for if you can't get smarter then it surely follows that ...

*   obstacles and other challenges expose lack of ability;

*   mistakes too are a function of an inherent ineptitude and klutziness;

*   hard work is merely a poor substitute for natural ability ('He's not that bright – he's just a hard worker');

*   constructive feedback hits at one's essential being – if feedback can't grow brain cells it's irrelevant to progress and future success;

*   more successful peers are genetically blessed and reflect adversely on others' more modest achievements ('Salieri syndrome', from the film *Amadeus*).

By contrast, other people believe that ability is a fluid, malleable quality that can wax or wane depending on the prevailing conditions. These are people with *growth mindsets*. They tend to respond very differently, as they're always on the lookout for learning opportunities which might grow their abilities:

*   obstacles and other challenges create opportunities for new learning, not just for practising old learning;

*   mistakes invite reflection, processing and new strategies – ie new learning;

*   hard work is where it's at ('Genius is one per cent inspiration and ninety-nine per cent perspiration' – Thomas Edison);

*   constructive feedback enhances performance – what's not to like?

*   more successful peers are a source of inspiration, role models and useful collaborators in learning.

There are roughly equal proportions of people with more or less fixed or growth mindsets, and a smaller proportion who have balanced or mixed mindsets (neither one nor the other, or fixed in some areas and growth in others). These proportions cut across age, social, intellectual, racial and gender groupings, although it does seem to be the case that if a high-achieving girl has a fixed mindset, she is even more vulnerable to crises of confidence and 'impostor syndrome' than a high-achieving boy with a fixed mindset – with all the attendant issues such as stress, depression, or panic. The reasons for this difference are likely to be complex and almost certainly implicate society in its differential treatment of and expectations for boys and girls.

It doesn't take much to see how important mindsets are to learner progress, especially when, as a teacher, you want your learners to take ownership of their own learning, to work increasingly without your constant prompting, urging and support, and with the ceiling on their achievements not so much lifted as removed. It's possible for a learner with a fixed mindset to do comfortably well in a system of low challenge, and indeed many learners leave the system each year with impressive qualifications and zero resourcefulness and resilience. If they have experienced 360-degree support, scaffolding and opportunity year on year, and consequently achieve highly without having had to acquire a mastery orientation to learning, their learning weaknesses will be exposed only when they *do* first encounter real challenges and threats to their self-image as capable, smart, high performers. For some this will be in the world of work: sales targets, demanding bosses, competitive colleagues. For others this might be at college or university: leading universities in the UK report exceptional demands on their counselling services by learners whose first experiences of failure lead to crippling over-reactions.

Recent research (eg Moser et al, 2011) is beginning to show just how – at a neural level – individuals with growth mindsets tend to identify, process and correct errors much more successfully than individuals with a fixed mindset, whose brains tend to shut down in response to error. For learners endorsing fixed notions of ability, error seems to be so shameful that denial and avoidance become the overriding reactions – definitely not the route to new learning!

Fortunately, given the salience of mindset to learning, mindsets can and do change. They are only beliefs after all, and beliefs are susceptible to many influences. Many of these influences are to be found in the classroom, and later chapters are explicit about the ways in which we can actively promote growth mindset messages and discourage the maintenance or development of fixed mindsets. In Chapter 5, for instance, we show how quality feedback and constructive criticism can nurture a desire to grow one's skills, whereas the most common and vacuous forms of praise and reward can inadvertently feed a fixed mindset. And in our next chapter we will show the value of encouraging in your learners the dispositions and mastery orientation that lead to autonomous inquiry.

What is essential is that you, as a teacher, seek at all times to root out the limiting beliefs that inhibit your own and your learners' learning development, and replace these with beliefs that don't vitiate – they vitalise. When you see yourself as a work in progress rather than the finished article, you will be able to look upon that disastrous lesson (which has a million manifestations but is the common experience of *every* teacher) with gentle eyes, as a marvellous opportunity to learn from your mistakes. You are not and don't need to be a 'naturally gifted teacher' – that mythic beast who springs forth fully formed at birth, just waiting for the years to pass before she can be unleashed on her first class. There lie monsters, which pounce viciously on your first failure and tempt you to pack it all in. There's a world of difference between the honest reflection and determination to try a new strategy next time (the mark of a growth mindset), and the self-flagellation, despair or temptation to cheat that marks out the response to failure of a fixed mindset. Take the honest road.

Things to try

» Critically reflect on your own beliefs about the malleability of intelligence. Do you have high expectations of all your learners and avoid placing limits on individuals? How is this expressed through your classroom practice? Do some further reading at least of open access online resources on mindset and its classroom applications. Good starting points are available at: http://mindsetonline.com/changeyourmindset/firststeps/ and http://learningwithoutlimits.educ.cam.ac.uk/.

» Consider the way of reframing errors, mistakes and failures that the musician and conductor Benjamin Zander writes about (Zander and Zander, 2000): in response to your own or a learner's errors, make your initial response 'How fascinating!' or 'How interesting!'

» Show your class some slides of neural connections in the brain (there are some stunning images online), and explain how these strengthen and multiply in response to deliberate practice – and that there are no known limits to the connections they can make.

» Ask your class to recount experiences they've had of struggling to achieve something (however modest), but getting there eventually through persistence, grit and resilience. Then ask them if they think they've changed their brains in some way – how?

» Try to remember if you've ever been labelled in some deterministic way – for example, as 'bright', 'slow', 'clumsy', 'sporty', 'tone-deaf', etc. What was the effect it had – and has – on you? Ask your learners about this, and ask them to point out if you ever lapse into lazy labels.

» Imagine you've been commissioned to create explicitly growth-mindset stickers. Instead of smiley faces, 'Well done!' and 'Great reader!', what could they say to focus the learner on learning dispositions? One of the authors was commissioned to do just this, and when he shared these with a class of 11-year-olds, one of his new stickers was devastatingly savaged by a learner – 'I'm gritty'. Consider why the learner was correct, and how this sticker could be improved (hint: think transient behaviour, not permanent identity).

TEACHERS' WORKPLACE LEARNING

Developing teacher identity

So, beliefs versus ability! We wonder if you really recognise this teacher dilemma? We are all subjected to strong cultural influences, often entangled with social class, asserting that nature, not nurture, decides the success of our learners. In this section we move on to consider *your* professional learning as a teacher. To what extent do you feel one or two of your colleagues, who seem to be really effective in the classroom, were simply born as 'natural' teachers? Perhaps you should ask them how they got to be the teachers they are now, and question them about mindset. Meanwhile, do you sometimes wonder if you are really 'cut out' to be a teacher, especially if you have recently had a difficult lesson or incident with a learner?

The good news in this chapter is that becoming a great teacher is mostly about your attitude, determination, reflexivity, effort and resilience. You can develop a growth mindset in relation to your professional learning. Many different kinds of people become great teachers, from many different backgrounds and starting points. There is a big challenge, because becoming a great teacher is a complex process and one for the long haul. You could use this book as a tool to challenge your thinking and support your development. Look for and celebrate your progress in the journey of becoming a great teacher.

In addition to your beliefs about your own learning, it is important to reflect on your beliefs about children's ability and work to free yourself from outdated ideas of fixed ability and of ability-labelling children as 'bright', 'average' or 'less able'. The 'Learning without Limits' approach sets out a convincing argument that teacher beliefs are a crucial element of the learning environment in schools and impact significantly on the learner identities that children develop (Hart et al, 2004; Swann et al, 2012). Identity is an important and powerful concept for learners and also for teachers, so as you read on we ask you to reflect on your own developing teacher identity and consider where it came from and how it is continuing to develop.

Teacher identity

Identity is an important concept for beginning teachers because teaching is mainly about relationships. Identities are a major influence on how we see ourselves and how we might understand others. So it is important for you to consider and become aware of your developing professional identity as a teacher. In practice, it is helpful to consider multiple identities because most thinkers on identity recognise the interwoven nature of different dimensions or strands to our identity. Identity is a complex and contested concept, but we will develop a working definition here for the purpose of helping you to consider your early development as a teacher.

Figure 2.1 *Multiple identity trajectories as intertwined narratives developing over time*

Identity may be defined as a self-generated and evolving narrative that we tell about ourselves, about who we are. For example, one day your professional identity narrative may include the phrase 'I am an effective teacher' or even 'I am an inspirational teacher'. Of course, if questioned about our professional identity as a teacher we may tell a story that is not completely aligned with the reality of our classroom or the views of our learners. For example, a colleague might claim to be very learner-focused but in observing their teaching you may find that they lecture quite a bit and the lesson is very teacher-dominated. Notice in this discussion the blurring of the boundaries between identity and practice. This is because our preferred definition of identity is influenced by a sociocultural perspective where identity and practice are closely related and the relationship between them is continually negotiated (Wenger, 1998). Who I am is at least partly determined by what I do.

Identity is not a fixed story but is dynamic and ever-changing, so that we are maintaining the narrative from day to day. For example, even very experienced and reasonably successful teachers will occasionally have a poor lesson with a challenging class on a wet and windy afternoon and could easily find themselves thinking 'Why am I in teaching? I am just not very good at it ... maybe I should be doing something else?' However, the very next morning, perhaps a great lesson, or a conversation with an individual child or some feedback from a parent or colleague might restore their belief and excitement about teaching and about themselves as teachers. These kinds of critical incidents, and an ability to bounce back from knocks or build on successes, influence the developing trajectory of professional identity, giving it shape and direction.

Identity is not just one story but is actually likely to be several intertwined narratives with cross-overs, blurred boundaries and possibly even contradictions between them. You may have one or more personal identity trajectories as well as one or more professional ones. For example, you may be a daughter or son, a parent, carer or friend and so on. Some of these personal identities will strongly shape the kind of teacher you wish to be. The image of a traditional braided rope helps to capture the idea of inter-twined identity trajectories (Figure 2.1) and in this case it illustrates some of the identities recognised by Julie, a young beginning teacher. Imagine the 'rope' in action and the tensions within it as the different strands of Julie's identify intertwine and rub against each other.

Julie is a new teacher in her first year since qualifying and sees herself as a 'caring' teacher. However, her teacher identity is related to some of her other identity strands. Her first degree was in biochemistry and this background as a scientist means that in learning to be a teacher she is engaging with new ideas from the social sciences and has to widen her appreciation of what constitutes valid research evidence. To some extent Julie would admit that as a scientist she tends towards the nature side of the old 'nature versus nurture' debate. She might be aware of the evidence from the field of epigenetics though, and now sees nature and nurture in a third way – as inextricably enmeshed. Her main hobby is playing the guitar and this rather tentative identity as a 'musician' currently feels quite separate from her identity as a teacher. This seems a shame because in playing the guitar she strongly recognises that practice, at the edge of her ability, will enable her to reach a very high standard. Julie is in a steady relationship but is planning to establish herself as a teacher for three or four years before thinking about getting married or having children of her own. She is uncertain about how long it will take for her to feel established and to have made a firm foundation in her career as a teacher.

From this brief example of Julie's identity we hope you can see how your personal identity is likely to become interwoven with who you are as a teacher and with the kind of teacher that you want to be. You might usefully reflect on the strands of your own developing identity and consider how that affects your practice in the classroom. To what extent does your mindset play a part in your developing identity trajectory as a teacher? Is there a limit to what you might achieve as a teacher or might effort and practice enable you to become an inspirational teacher and school leader?

In defining identity there is one more aspect to consider. Etienne Wenger developed the idea of 'paradigmatic identity role models', by which he means that in a particular workplace there may be one or two colleagues who are seen as high-performing and their way of being might inform your ambitions for development (Wenger, 1998). As you look around your school or other educational setting you may well see individual teachers that you respect. There is something about their practice and their way of 'being' a teacher that impresses or even inspires you and they are highly valued and seen as outstanding within the school. These paradigmatic identity role models may not always consist of just one teacher; you may identify elements of different teachers that seem impressive. These teachers are effective within the school or other educational workplace setting in which you are based and in that way are particularly respected. This captures the meaning of 'paradigmatic', in that this is the kind of teacher that is particularly valued within the particular workplace setting. Hopefully you will not be too 'star-struck' – you need to question the impact of these teachers on their learners. However, you may be able to form a paradigmatic identity role model – imagine a kind of hybrid ideal teacher – informed by these impressive teachers. You should seek out these role models and question why these characters might represent the kind of teacher you aspire to be and how they got to be that way. Developing a 'mission' in this way, an outline of the kind of teacher you wish to become, is a useful strategy to help you through the inevitable knock-backs that you will experience during your journey of becoming a great teacher. Writing down your mission and then planning some time each week to spend on 'mission-critical' activity is a useful way to ensure that you continue to develop despite the busyness of school life (Covey, 2004).

Personal history

A key challenge for teachers is that we all have a personal history as learners. This will usually be a mixture of schooling and higher education and altogether it adds up to thousands of hours spent observing teachers. The problem is that these many hours of observation were from the perspective of a learner, and very often from the perspective of a successful learner. If you are lucky you may also have fond memories of at least one inspirational teacher. Consider this reflection from one of the authors of this book:

> *For myself, without doubt, the inspirational teacher who influenced my whole life was Mr Pender. Mr Pender was an outstanding geography teacher who taught me at Royal Liberty School, Gidea Park, from 1971 to 1978. He kept me in touch with school when I was in danger of going off the rails. I found his enthusiasm for geography infectious and decided I had to go to university and continue to study the subject beyond school. I guess one risk is that during my 35 years working in education, as a school teacher and then as a university lecturer, I have simply been trying my best to become Mr Pender and do what Mr Pender did, or at least what I thought Mr Pender was doing from my position as a teenage learner. Hopefully, however, I have been inspired and influenced by Mr Pender but inevitably have found my own way to be the teacher that I am today.*

Perhaps you weren't fortunate enough to be inspired by a particular teacher, or perhaps you have several great teachers that you can recall influencing you. In either case it is important to reflect on your generalised view of what makes a good teacher. Consider your mindset in relation to your own learning as teacher. Do you believe that practice at the edge of your ability will enable you to become the kind of teacher you wish to be? Or do you feel that you have a certain ability as a teacher and need to defend that and not take too many risks?

All of these memories ingrained into our beings are, of course, of great value in becoming a teacher and may be summed up as our 'personal history of learning and teaching'. However, there are many pathways to becoming an inspirational teacher. It is important to consider the influence of our personal educational histories and to remain self-aware. We mustn't fall into the trap of assuming that all of our learners think the same way about school as we did at their age.

Above all, it is important to focus on the impact of our teaching on our learners and to be prepared to question the underlying assumptions we may have about what makes a good teacher. This kind of 'unfreezing' of existing ideas is very challenging and may lead to a period of uncertainty, but it is an essential part of the learning process.

During your career as a teacher it is important that you retain a habit of questioning your personal assumptions, especially when you move schools or get promoted to formal leadership roles. Critical awareness of your history as a learner, of your developing identity as a teacher and of your current repertoire of teaching strategies will help you to adapt quickly to new contexts or policy change in a way that prioritises children's learning and is collaborative and likely to carry colleagues with you. In order to contribute fully as a professional teacher, it is essential that you engage with, but critically question and challenge, conceptions of 'good practice' as proposed by your mentor, your team, your school leaders, the governors or company that oversee your school, published texts such as the one you are reading, the school inspection body and above all your government, as represented by the teaching agency or education department. Think of your professional learning as a social interplay between these different influences, including local practical wisdom of teachers in your school and the public, published knowledge of theory, research evidence, professional guidance and policy. You will need to proactively manage that learning interplay as it involves relationships, emotions, power and identity.

When you tell social acquaintances that you are a teacher they will sometimes offer their opinions, based on their own personal histories, of what makes a great teacher. Even government ministers in charge of your national education system have been to school themselves and have a personal history of learning and teaching. Based on this they often think that they know what makes a great teacher and devise national policy on little more than this 'common sense'. Surrounded by all these 'experts' with often conflicting opinions, it is important for you to position yourself in relation to the wider policy context and aim to contribute to the health and development of the teaching profession. At the very least you need to position your classroom, your teaching team, your school and its community within the wider policy and social framework. Putting your head in the sand in relation to the big picture is likely to restrict your growth as a critical, thinking professional and your ability to make a significant contribution. Consider subscribing to the professional press or to professional websites that will help you to keep up to date on educational policy and be reasonably well informed about the bigger picture. But do also remember to enjoy the contribution you are able to make locally and to manage the demands on yourself.

Resilience

The metaphor of professional learning as 'interplay' captures some idea of the power involved in teachers' professional lives. Handling relationships and learning in such a role will be enhanced by a willingness to reflect critically and to develop self-awareness – but this kind of professional growth requires *resilience*.

Teacher resilience may be defined as the ability to recover quickly when new challenges arise or when you make mistakes (Gu and Day, 2007). In this paper based on a large study of 300 teachers over a three-year period, these authors argue that a sense of vocation – a commitment to improving children's learning and lives – will help you to be resilient. They also emphasise teacher self-efficacy, your belief that you can continue to improve as a teacher and make a positive contribution. Resilience is a disposition that needs to be developed and strengthened across personal and professional aspects of your life. It is supported by positive emotional experiences, supportive relationships with peers and a positive workplace environment. We argue in this book that even if your workplace is challenging it is possible for you to take proactive steps to allow yourself to be a learner as well as a teacher. One key step is to find yourself a critical friend or professional buddy, even if they are not in the same school as you.

You will need to call on your resilience during your entire career, but it is particularly important early on when you are very likely to make frequent mistakes, for example, in relationships with children or colleagues, and even mundane events such as getting some subject matter wrong may feel really disheartening. Perhaps retaining a sense of humour and proportion will also be important. An element of resilience is required for professional workplace learning in order to think reflectively, to accept and act on feedback and to bounce back from setbacks. You might forgive colleagues when they are perhaps not as supportive as they might be. You will need to try and make the most of mistakes by learning from them. Having at least one critical friend with whom you can share your experiences will be a crucial support during tough times.

We are arguing here that becoming an effective teacher means developing yourself as a resilient learner with a growth mindset. If you are determined and willing to practise enough, that is to practise at the edge of your current ability, then we can assure you that you will become more 'intelligent' as a teacher and therefore more effective. To practise at the edge of your ability you will find it helpful to set goals, but they need to be the right kind of goals.

Setting mastery goals, rather than performance goals, will help you to make progress in becoming the teacher you want to be. People with mastery goals are determined to *improve* something, whereas people with performance goals are far more interested in *proving* something. For example, rather than focusing on avoiding mistakes and getting a high-scoring lesson evaluation after being observed by a teacher educator or headteacher, as a mastery-oriented learner you will aim to improve a particular aspect of your teaching such as questioning skills. Rather than 'playing it safe' in planning for a lesson observation you might plan and test an innovative strategy and use the observer as a classroom coach to help evaluate and refine that approach. Your mastery goals may originate from previous feedback, from your own evaluation of your teaching or from your ambitions in relation to your developing identity as a teacher.

Formal teaching standards from your government, or provided as part of your teacher education programme, may also help you to identify core practices of a teacher that you wish to target for improvement. However, it is important that you treat such published sets of standards as just one debatable framework, produced by a committee and most useful for provoking professional conversations rather than as a checklist of competences. Questioning such official policy documents and how they are used by teacher educators and managers is part of becoming a professional. Strict unquestioning compliance with official codes is a sign of a technician, not of a professional teacher who will contribute to educational development and enhancement of the profession.

The lessons of mindset include setting high challenge but focusing feedback on progress, effort and the strategies used. Apply these ideas to the self-management of your own professional development as a teacher. Learn from your mistakes and celebrate the fact that you are making errors because it means you are pushing on the boundaries of your current ability as a teacher and therefore maximising your professional learning. At the same time, view managing effort and avoiding exhaustion as a professional competence. In your learning remember to seek out interplay between horizontal and vertical domains of learning so that you are seeking out published research evidence and professional guidance to help understand your successes and failures in developing the practical wisdom of a teacher. At the same time do allow that you are likely to reach full effectiveness as a teacher only after five to eight years of experience, so try to enjoy the journey rather than getting frustrated that your practice is not perfect.

To sum up, this section has argued that developing a strong awareness of your identity as a teacher, including consideration of your personal educational history, will help you to build resilience. Above all, in developing your teacher identity, nurture a growth mindset and believe that determination and practice will allow you to grow into the teacher you aspire to be. Consider how your growth mindset about your own learning is related to your beliefs in relation to your learners and is clearly reflected in your classroom practice.

Things to try

» *Reflect on a teacher who was an inspiration to you. What was it about their practice or their being that so impressed you? Were you uniquely affected, or do you think that teacher had a similar effect on many others?*

» *Consider an issue or incident arising from your recent practice in school and ask yourself: How does it connect to my beliefs about good teaching? What kind of teacher do my current learners need? What are the local ways of working on this issue within my school? How is that influenced by the wider educational framework? What do professional guidance and research evidence suggest? What kind of teacher do I want to be and what is a practical first step I can make towards this ambition?*

» *Reflect on your most recent day or week in school in relation to your own resilience. What challenges your own resilience? And what develops your resilience? You might think about being well organised, managing time, building effective relationships and nurturing your own growth mindset about becoming a great teacher. How strong is your self-awareness? What about not taking feedback too personally? How well do you maintain your sense of humour and proportion? How well do you manage your work–life balance? Consider how developing a clear mission and a strong sense of the kind of teacher you want to become will help to strengthen your resilience.*

Reflections on Amy's poetry lesson

Before reading on it is worth pausing now to reflect critically on Amy's lesson, presented at the beginning of this chapter. Based on what you have read about ability and mindset, and about teacher identity, this is a chance for you to deepen your response to Amy's lesson, and crucially to consider this response in relation to your own practice in your current workplace.

1. **Is there a sense that Amy's expectations of this class are lower because of the low ability of the set, and the fact she has been told they will not secure a C grade? How far are her expectations borne out of the view of others in the school?**

Amy has taken at face value the view, aired by another teacher in her department, that the class has switched off because the learners realise they are not expected to achieve the magic C grade. If it is true that the learners have switched off, then this is a difficult situation, and one which Amy needs to tackle. However, the first step for Amy is not to accept this opinion which has been shared with her, but to think for herself and try not to let this view colour her relationship with the class. Remember, it is not the class teacher who held this view, but another colleague, so it may be particularly necessary to exercise caution: we know the class teacher has an excellent relationship with the class, so if Amy were to come along with a more negative initial view, she could be getting off on the wrong foot entirely. Amy is working in a good, friendly department and she will learn a great deal from her colleagues, but she also needs to maintain her own subjectivity and judge key matters for herself. We learnt in this chapter that what someone believes about ability is more significant educationally than the ability itself, so perhaps this is a perfect opportunity for Amy, as a teacher new to the class, as she has the chance to show them that she is one of the teachers who believes in them. This might get things off to the best possible start, as the learners may respond positively to the fact that their new teacher believes in them. Perhaps Amy needs to make it her priority to share those positive beliefs with the class, which may be in both explicit and implicit ways (explicit in that she shares her positive expectations with them and lets them know she believes they can succeed; more implicit in the types of activity she chooses to use with them).

It is commonplace now for schools to put a lot of emphasis on predicted grades, and to have very well-established and dominant systems that ensure teachers, and often learners themselves, are making regular reference to predicted grades and using these to influence their planning. Clearly, a new teacher is not in a strong position to question the expectations that such systems may promote. We are not saying here that every child in Amy's class is going to achieve the very highest grade, but what we did learn in this chapter is that targets and predicted grades are not 'a window into the future', so Amy would be well served to treat the predictions here with caution, and not let knowledge of them dominate what she chooses to do with the class.

2. **To what extent does Amy seem open to developing her own curriculum subject knowledge around poetry? What is the relationship between her longstanding disenchantment with and avoidance of poetry at school and university and her perceived lack of ability to teach it?**

No matter how glittering an individual's academic career, we all have 'blind spots' – areas of study we enjoyed less than others, skills we found difficult to pick up, topics we viewed as more difficult than others. If we examine our feelings about our own specialist areas of curriculum subject knowledge, we are likely to find something which allows us to empathise with Amy's disenchantment with poetry. In Amy's case, however, we can see the danger of these lingering beliefs we have about ourselves and our prior learning and knowledge: Amy's views of teaching this curriculum area are immediately coloured by her own more negative memories of her prior learning. It seems likely that this disenchantment (and the associated lack of learning opportunities to develop her skills as a result of avoiding the area) will colour the way she communicates with the class about poetry. When people talk about inspirational teachers in their past, they often mention how much a teacher loved a topic, their infectious enthusiasm for it. Amy's caution seems to be the opposite of that, and it is difficult to see how she will enthuse a class about poetry when she feels so ambivalent about it herself. We get a sense of Amy's fixed mindset here, however – she can articulate her negativity, but she isn't displaying a desire to overcome this, to fix what might be broken, to give it another go. It is true that she has more work to do in the planning of the lesson because she has to address her own subject knowledge and her feelings about that subject knowledge, but this is surely the first step she needs to take to make a success of not only this series of lessons, but the other poetry lessons she will teach in her career. There is a short- and long-term investment for Amy if she decides to read and listen to more poetry with an open and inquiring mind.

3.   **To what extent can you connect with Amy's feelings about the boy who offered to bring in an ancestor's war medal – the tension between curriculum progression and honouring a learner's engagement?**

It is easy to read about this lesson and think, 'Well, of course she should make time to let the student bring in and talk about the medal.' However, this is a prime example of a situation where the demands of the real world clash with ideals for a lesson or for learning, and it's easier said than done to suggest that time can simply be found. Such situations are common-place and are a real source of tension for teachers. It is far from unusual to hear a teacher say something like, 'If we had more time, of course I'd do such and such', or 'I'd love to try a more creative approach, but unfortunately the curriculum/exam specification just doesn't allow it.' It would be easy for us, when writing a book like this, to declare that you simply must find the time to allow for flexibility that will enable such moments of learner engagement to emerge. We know that there are numerous pressures on time in schools, particularly for exam classes, and we are realistic that not every opportunity can be taken. However, we would encourage you to question whether Amy, if she were flexible enough to respond to the opportunity presented, could in fact deepen the learning not only of this individual boy, but of other learners in the class. For example she could allow him to bring in the medal next lesson, spend ten minutes letting him talk about it, relate it back to the learning on the poem in this lesson, encourage discussion, and emphasise the relevance of the poem to students' families and lives now. Amy is in fact supposed to be teaching the 'unseen' poem, so if she branched out and spent time looking at a non-anthology poem on the subject of war that would be time well invested. This could do so much to strengthen the real learning. This is not an idealistic stance, it is a realistic one – students are required to show a personal response to poetry in their English exams, and this is a perfect opportunity to invite such responses. Moving away from the specifics of this lesson, we would encourage you not to let the pressures of exams, time or schemes of work blind you to opportunities that may allow remarkable learning to take place. Of course, the real-world pressures need to be respected, but it's all too easy not to see the wood for the trees.

4. **How far do you think Amy's aspirations for the lesson are limited by her own feelings about poetry and her ability to teach it? She says she is 'pretty pleased' with the lesson at the end. Do you think it is reasonable she should think this (she does overcome some major worries about her ability to work with this class), or should she have higher expectations for herself, and consequently for the lesson?**

Though we have only this short scenario to go on, it does not seem that Amy is approaching this lesson with a growth mindset. She has decided at the outset that she still has negative feelings about poetry herself, stemming from school, and it seems she adopted avoidance tactics during her degree, so she has never given herself the opportunity to change that fixed view. This seems a shame, because she does have a clear personal response to the poem and sees that it is a moving war poem, and she reads about the poem and understands something of the way it works. So this suggests she could develop a more positive response. In the same way that most of us have met inspirational teachers in our school experience, so most of us have less positive memories of school also. It seems a shame to let a negative learning experience from years ago still colour our impressions of something in adulthood, particularly if this is an area we need to develop as part of our professional skills. In fact, Amy could see this as a chance to change her view of poetry, to set herself the challenge of reading more poetry, reading about poetry, going to poetry readings, watching poetry performances on the internet – to embrace the fact this is a less robust area of her subject knowledge and to do something about that, to be even more determined to be a good teacher of poetry so she does not pass on that more negative view from her own school days. Learners who are developing or strengthening a growth mindset look for opportunities to grow their abilities, and this is an ideal prompt for professional learning for Amy.

This is not, however, to ignore the fact Amy rises to some different challenges during this lesson: she is unsure about teaching this exam class, largely because of worries about motivation and behaviour, and she is right to celebrate some success here and to allow this to help her increase her confidence. So it would be churlish to suggest that she should not be pleased with some aspects of the lesson. Yet, there is no doubt she could have higher expectations of herself and therefore of the class. If we remember that mistakes invite reflection, then we may feel a little more ready to push ourselves further in realising what is possible.

5. **Amy is supposed to be teaching the students about the 'unseen' poetry element of the exam, but she ends up covering a poem from their anthology, and seems to forget about the initial idea for the lesson. Why do you think this is?**

If we look a little more at the detail of the lesson, we will see that Amy has in fact missed entirely what she set out to do here. She has covered one of the set anthology poems, but seems to have forgotten that her initial brief was to look at unseen poems. This is another example of where Amy perhaps takes the guidance she is given too much at face value. The students need to develop their skills in dealing with poems they have not come across before, and it is arguably not ideal that a poem they need to know very well indeed is being used to teach a different skill. Although there are undoubtedly time pressures, the expectations of the students seem to have been lowered here. The class teacher may be an excellent English teacher, but she is also under a great deal of time pressure. While the schedule for the class means Amy is also affected by time pressures, this is an opportunity for Amy to work together with her colleague to evaluate how the poetry is being taught and perhaps for Amy to suggest something new.

There is an opportunity here for Amy to be more ambitious with her ideas for the lesson. Approaching this with a growth mindset, she would question the way she is presenting the students with poetry, and would think creatively about ways in which she can expand the students' understanding as well as her own. Step one may be to use a poem which is genuinely 'unseen' and not from the published anthology, even though the students do need to study those poems for the exam. She could select a poem that she thinks will surprise and intrigue the students. Rather than asking them to identify poetic features as a 'way in', she could allow students the space to have a personal response to the poem. She could prioritise the poem itself, giving students a chance to read it more than once, and also perhaps to listen to it using freely available internet sources such as the Poetry Archive (www.poetryarchive.org). Although she and the class are working under time pressures, the fact is that these students will sit an exam where they have to write about a poem they have never seen before without the guidance of a teacher to help them find 'the right answer'; in fact, there is unlikely to be a 'right answer'. Above all, she needs to increase the students' confidence in reading and writing about poetry. A short-term solution is to spoon-feed them information about poems, but a longer-term view builds their own abilities to respond with genuine understanding. In your own teaching you will, of course, have different areas of curriculum focus, but you will be able to apply Amy's situation to something from your own practice. What makes this lesson of Amy's a useful one to think about is that the need for students to think for themselves cannot be an optional extra or something which is thought of as a luxury, easily sacrificed because of time pressures. Although we believe that independent learning and independent thought are necessary in all curriculum areas, in this particular example to succeed in this assessment, the students *have* to be able to *think* for themselves. Think of a subject area with which you are involved where the students need to be able to think for themselves to succeed in an area of assessment. Consider whether you are embedding this skill in the learning, and consider whether it is embedded in your own approach and your own thinking about the lesson focus.

In fact, Amy does get a highly personal and heartfelt response from one student who clearly understands something important about the poem as he wants to bring in his great-grandfather's medal. Unfortunately, the time pressures dominate Amy's thinking to such an extent that she does not feel able to capitalise on this development. It serves as a reminder that the students are capable of having a personal response and deeper understanding, and this could be just the thing on which Amy can capitalise to help the students see the power of the poem and its relevance to their lives now.

6.   **Amy is following guidance from the experienced teacher. It may be very tricky for a new teacher to go against the established ways of working in a teaching team. Do you think it is realistic for Amy to think for herself and even challenge the practical wisdom of the experienced teacher?**

There is no doubt that this is a tricky area. It is very difficult indeed to walk into a new professional situation and to challenge received wisdom, and this may not always be desirable. Amy has to work with her new colleagues and build positive relationships with them (and we will think more about this in Chapter 6 when we discuss collaborative learning). We also need to be mindful of the fact that individual teachers may also be representing very well-established whole-school policy and practice. Frequently, however, established teachers are very keen to hear new ideas and approaches from beginning teachers with whom they share their classes. This is an exciting part of mentoring new teachers, and one which many more experienced practitioners relish as a part of their job. Amy should feel confident about thinking for herself and making suggestions about how she may like to approach something slightly differently: in many schools and departments her ideas would be gratefully received and considered. The best practice in our schools often comes from teams of people who are keen to share ideas and approaches with each other.

What it is probably reasonable to hope for here is that a middle ground can be sought. Amy can listen to advice from various people, and can reflect on what she will prioritise as she finds her own way forward. Any new teacher needs to have the confidence to suggest some ideas and approaches of their own. We can also think about ways in which Amy can be pro-active in seeking out colleagues whose practice will help her develop her own. We learnt that learners with growth mindsets seek out more successful peers who can act as inspiration and be role models. Amy could talk to as many members of the department as possible, as well as looking to external contacts to find out about approaches to exam poetry and to teaching exam classes, and can offer some of these ideas back to the teaching team. Successful schools will be open to new suggestions, as well as being open to sharing their established expertise.

7. **Amy's approach to the poem allows the class to have some notes about the poem, and to identify some 'features' of the poem (alliteration and imagery), so there is some tangible evidence the students have done something. Is there any evidence the students have *learnt* something, however?**

It is very easy to fool ourselves that learning has taken place because the students have 'done' something and there is a tangible 'product' produced in the lesson (in this case, some notes on the poem). If the students have been on-task and engaged in doing something, this can confirm our belief that learning has taken place. However, it is not always the case that any meaningful or lasting learning has occurred. Amy perhaps should reflect on the level of challenge in this lesson. In her planning stage, it may have been useful for her to question whether the central tasks in the lesson are encouraging deep learning and understanding, or whether they have merely short-term gains. If she believes that she and the students are capable of this deeper understanding, then this will have a knock-on effect on what she wants the students to do in the lesson, and will influence the ways in which she may judge whether learning has taken place by the end of the lesson.

This is a lesson which may succeed on one level – most students can identify some of the features of the poem. However, it is more than an idealistic notion to want students to have a deeper, more meaningful sense of the power of such a text. Students must be able to comment on the effect of writing, and in order to do this, they need to develop a personal response to what they are reading and hearing. Examination bodies themselves are encouraging teachers to get beyond a utilitarian approach. Amy's development of a growth mindset for her students, and indeed for herself, could perhaps be predicated on an attempt to engage the students in the horror and tragedy which permeate this poem.

Things to try

» *Consider your planning of a lesson you have taught recently. You are likely to have written out two or three intended learning outcomes for the lesson and designed one or two learning activities for learners to tackle. You may have also identified some success criteria to share with the learners and planned this lesson within a sequence that aims for progression in learning. First, reflect on the level of challenge expressed in the intended learning outcomes and activities – to what extent were learners really stretched during the lesson and sufficiently engaged to be working at the limit of their current ability? Second, reflect on the kinds of feedback the learners received during and after the lesson on the work they produced – to what extent did it focus on the effort they made and the strategies they used? Third, reflect on the messages your learners are receiving from you personally – to what extent do they feel you have belief in and commitment to their development? Overall, apply our key question: What is my impact on learning and learners?*

» *If you are teaching a class which is being externally assessed, double-check the specifications, assessment guidelines and examiners' reports. Look for places where deeper learning and understanding is being tested (not necessarily just for the highest grades), and consider how this is evident in your teaching approaches.*

Chapter 2 summary

This chapter has focused on the dilemma 'belief versus ability'. This dilemma creates cognitive dissonance for many teachers because it contradicts long and widely held assumptions in education and more widely in society about natural ability, genetic inheritance and social class.

Learning power

- Learners with a fixed mindset tend to defend their current levels of ability, while learners with a growth mindset believe in learning through effort and practice. Consider your beliefs about your learners and how these are communicated in the expectations you set and the feedback you give.

- As a teacher you can nurture growth mindset in learners by providing feedback on effort and strategies, by helping them to develop their thinking dispositions and by teaching learners (and their parents/carers) about how the brain works.

- A positive learning environment in your classroom means high challenge, but combined with collaboration, trust and a view that making mistakes, and even failing a challenging task, are opportunities for learning.

Teachers' workplace learning

- As a teacher you have the power to strongly influence the mindset of your learners, whatever the wider context within which you are working. Adopt strategies in lesson planning and feedback that help to nurture a growth mindset in your learners.

- Aim to develop a growth mindset with regard to your own professional learning. This means believing that you will become smarter as a teacher through sustained effort and practice that pushes at the boundaries of your current knowledge and skills.

- Build a mission statement and a strong identity story about what kind of teacher you are and want to become. This will help to build your resilience and ability to bounce back from knocks along the way.

- Acknowledge that your history as a learner shapes your conception of what a good teacher is and consider this influence carefully. Seek out great teachers and use them as identity role models. Consider how your teacher identity is interwoven with your other identity strands and be sure to set aside time and effort for those other parts of who you are and want to be.

Taking it further

- On behalf of your current and future learners, take your own professional learning seriously by establishing an ambitious teacher identity – who you are and who you want to be as a teacher. Identify your current strengths and your areas for development and set targets for aspects of teaching you wish to master.

- Find out more about mindset theory and consider the implications for the level of challenge you set for all learners, your design of learning activities including formative assessment and your use of feedback. Good starting points include the Teachers' Pocketbook on mindset theory (Hymer and Gershon, 2014) and Carole Dweck's accessible book (2006).

- Investigate the development of thinking dispositions within your own practice so that you are asking parts of the key question: 'What is my impact on learning and learners?' The *Dispositions* text is a good starting point for further reading but consider what foothold, if any, dispositional learning has in your current school and maybe start from there (Costa and Kallick, 2014).

- Read more on malleable conceptions of intelligence. A useful book by Sternberg and Grigorenko (2007) provides guidance on lessons that will develop the 'practical intelligence' of your learners.

References

Claxton, G. (2002) *Building Learning Power*. Bristol: TLO.

Costa, A. L. and Kallick, B. (2014) *Dispositions: Reframing Teaching and Learning*. London: Sage.

Covey, S. R. (2004) *The 7 Habits of Highly Effective People: Powerful Lessons in Personal Change*. London: Simon & Schuster.

Dweck, C. S. (2000) *Self Theories: Their Role in Motivation, Personality and Development*. Philadelphia, PA: Psychology Press.

Dweck, C. S. (2006) *Mindset: The New Psychology of Success*. New York: Random House.

Ericsson, K. A. (2009) *Development of Professional Expertise: Toward Measurement of Expert Performance and Design of Optimal Learning Environments*. Cambridge: Cambridge University Press.

Gardner, H. (1984) *Frames of Mind*. London: Fontana.

Gu, Q. and Day, C. (2007) Teachers Resilience: A Necessary Condition for Effectiveness. *Teaching and Teacher Education*, 23(8), pp 1302–316.

Hart, S., Dixon, A., Drummond, M. J. and McIntyre, D. (2004) *Learning without Limits*. Maidenhead: Open University Press.

Hymer, B. and Gershon, M. (2014) *Growth Mindset Pocketbook*. Alresford: Teachers' Pocketbooks.

Klenowski, V. (2009) Assessment for Learning Revisited: An Asia-Pacific Perspective. *Assessment in Education: Principles, Policy and Practice*, 16(3), pp 263–86.

Marzano, R. J., Pickering, D. J. and Pollock, J. E. (2001) *Classroom Instruction That Works: Research-Based Strategies for Increasing Student Achievement*. Alexandria, VA: ASCD.

Moser, J. S., Schroder, H. S., Heeter, C., Moran, T. P. and Lee, Y. H. (2011) Mind Your Errors: Evidence for a Neural Mechanism Linking Growth Mind-Set to Adaptive Posterror Adjustments. *Psychological Science*, 22(12), pp 1484–9.

Nuthall, G. (1999) Learning How to Learn. *International Journal of Educational Research*, 31 (3), pp 141–256.

Perkins, D. N. (1995) *Outsmarting IQ: The Emerging Science of Learnable Intelligence*. New York: The Free Press.

Sharron, H. (1994) *Changing Children's Minds*. Birmingham: Imaginative Minds.

Sternberg, R. J. (1997) *Successful Intelligence: How Practical and Creative Intelligence Determine Success in Life*. New York: Penguin/Putnam.

Sternberg, R. J. and Grigorenko, E. L. (2007) *Teaching for Successful Intelligence: To Increase Student Learning and Achievement* (2nd edn). London: Sage.

Swann, M., Peacock, A., Hart, S. and Drummond, M. J. (2012) *Creating Learning without Limits*. Maidenhead: Open University Press.

Wenger, E. (1998) *Communities of Practice: Learning, Meaning, and Identity*. Cambridge: Cambridge University Press.

Zander, R. S. and Zander, B. (2000) *The Art of Possibility: Transforming Professional and Personal Life*. Boston: Harvard Business Review Press.

Chapter 3 Autonomy versus compliance

This chapter is about

- **the nature of autonomous learning and self-determination;**
- **how to encourage the development of self-regulated learners;**
- **reflection on your own learning, encouraging you to question the extent to which you are learning autonomously as a teacher.**

Introduction

This chapter addresses the need for your practice to be focused on the development of self-regulated learners. The teacher dilemma 'autonomy versus compliance' might seem rather challenging if you are a new teacher struggling to get your learners simply to do as they are told. Behaviour management is understandably a key focus for beginning teachers, but we will argue that by approaching from a stance that focuses on compliance you are likely to increase the pressure on yourself to perform. This might lead to a spiral of increasing teacher dominance of the classroom. Alternatively, by designing more open-ended tasks, asking learners to make choices and steer their own learning, it is possible to increase levels of engagement and give yourself as the teacher more time to deal one-to-one with learners who are struggling to engage and behave reasonably.

This chapter is also about developing yourself as a self-regulated learner. The dilemma 'autonomy versus compliance' might irritate you somewhat if you are being formally assessed as a teacher and feeling considerable pressure to conform to whatever local rules apply within your school about what a good teacher should be. We would argue that your professional responsibility and your continued learning require that you do not simply comply with local practical wisdom or policy but maintain a questioning stance and adopt the 'plan, do, reflect' approach of the self-regulated learner (Zimmerman, 2002).

CLASSROOM SCENARIO

Humza's mathematics lesson

I could not wait for the lesson to be over, but there were still 20 minutes to go. Not since my job in a call centre had I looked at the clock so intently, willing the second hand to double its speed. And at least in the call centre there weren't thirty 12-year-old students raising the roof. My only consolation was that I wasn't being observed, but I was still terrified that the head might come in and ask me exactly why I was showing children a mobile phone. School policy is very firmly not to allow phones in lessons, and here I was encouraging us to look at a phone and try out some of its features. This is my second placement though (on my one-year teacher education programme) and I wanted to try something different.

It had seemed like a good idea at the time, making maths authentic by using a real-world inquiry that is relevant to the students' lives. I'd read a blog post from a teacher who had tried teaching data handling through the use of mobile phones, and thought I would give it a go. This was a risk, though, because the end of term test would show up any failure on my part to 'cover' the topic effectively. Nonetheless, session one had gone OK. We had looked at a table of data about mobile phones from a comparison website, with information about contracts and 'pay as you go'. I'd spent an hour on YouTube looking at different phone adverts, and had chosen the one I thought would most appeal to them. I wanted to be careful, though, I know not everyone can afford a phone or is allowed one, so there was a danger I was opening up a can of worms. So I tried to word the inquiry question carefully, but to position it right up their street: what choices would a parent or carer make when choosing a phone for a young person? I had the first lesson planned to within an inch of its life, and it went like clockwork. They loved the whole idea, but I'd known the discussion could get out of hand. I had prepared a series of questions and a worksheet so they didn't get too carried away with chatting about the features of the latest smart phone, or the games they could play on one. I also didn't want to go too far down the parental control of the web route, as that's all a bit of a minefield, and in any case, I needed to keep the focus on the numbers. So we concentrated on considering the validity and accuracy of the data. Challenging talk, I know, but it was tailored to their needs, and they coped with it pretty well.

Lesson two involved students collecting survey data from each other, starting with the question 'What phone features would be most important to you when choosing a new phone?' In this 'market research' activity they had to collect different types of data from other students. For example: did they need unlimited texts? Would they need internet access? Was the look of the phone important? Then they had to present the data by using templates of a graph and a pie chart showing the relative popularity of various features. All this activity was intended to feed into lessons three and four, which were about interpreting results and drawing conclusions, with the aim of designing and costing a contract that would be most attractive to young people and using statistics selectively to 'pitch' their proposal to the mobile phone company.

It was lesson two that made me doubt my own sanity in coming up with this plan in the first place. I'd decided, against my better judgement, to demonstrate the key features of my own phone. The class teacher is quite creative and already does a lot of fun things with the class, so I felt as though I wanted to keep up with this approach, rather than rely on worksheets, which, to be honest, I'd seen quite a lot of on my first placement.

If I told you I spent an hour trying to decide on the learning outcomes, would you believe me? It's true, and I still don't know if I got them right. What I do know is that we hadn't met them by the end of lesson two. My school uses WALT (We Are Learning To …) and WILF (What I Am Looking For …), and there is a small whiteboard next to the smartboard with WALT and WILF permanently on it, and the students know they have to write that lesson's intended learning outcomes in their books at the start. So for lesson two, What We Are Learning To (WALT) was 'to present accurately different types of data' and What I Am Looking For (WILF) was 'interpreting statistics to support an argument'. I was also looking for a well-ordered lesson where my risky strategy did not blow up in my face, and though that's not what I wrote on the board, it was the main thing I was thinking about as I was waiting for them to come into the classroom. I felt the underlying concept I wanted students to engage with was that appropriately chosen graphs and statistics can be used to support an argument. But trying to get this into a WALT-able soundbite – that kept me up after bedtime, I can tell you. And I still had the awkward feeling that what I really wanted to do in that lesson was to develop the students' disposition to be 'questioning' or to be 'critical thinkers'. I wanted the students to not just accept statistics at face value, to not end up nagging their parents to buy a phone with a lousy contract.

So when they were getting over-excited, and when Sam and Chantelle were nearly coming to blows over the relative merits of Android over Apple, and when Sonny was out of his chair desperate to tell me that unlimited free texts is the only feature anyone needs to consider when choosing a contract, I seriously wished I'd stuck with the worksheet option. The quality of the written work at the end of the lesson was variable at best – most groups had not even started their graphs. I had a funny feeling that parents were going to be ringing up the next day asking why their kids had come home wanting to look at phone contracts and suggesting they should swap providers.

Too much noise. Not enough work done. Too much chat that was veering off task. A mistake to get my phone out. They were my assessments of the lesson, and I kept quiet about it in the staffroom, choosing to ignore the comment from a colleague who was teaching next door that I must have been doing drama and not maths if the noise level was anything to go by. My mentor was really pleased though, happy that I had taken a risk and done something which interested the students, and some of the students had told her that they'd enjoyed my lesson – but had they enjoyed it for the right reasons?

Questions about Humza's lesson

1. Do you think Humza is being too hard on himself? What are the positive features of the lessons?

2. What do you feel about the level of noise in a classroom; how does it relate to learning?

3. How do you feel about Humza's intended learning outcomes and what impact might they have on learning and learners? How open-ended are the learning outcomes that you use in your lesson planning?

4. Humza seems pretty certain the learning outcomes were not met in lesson two. How do you think Humza might change the lesson if he had the opportunity to teach it again?

5. Did Humza make a good decision to risk this authentic mathematics approach? Why not simply use worksheets with different examples of data and have students get plenty of practice in the data-handling tasks?

6. To what extent should Humza relax about this individual lesson which may have not gone quite according to plan? As one lesson within a sequence, is it possible for him to see it in a more positive light?

LEARNING POWER

The learning power of self-determination

It is easy, particularly in the early stages of your teaching career, to assume that student learning is happening when your learners are relatively quiet, comfortable and, in the educational cliché, 'on-task'. Surely that's better than seeing them loud, stressed and distracted? Well, quite possibly – but it's even more important to get a sense of what's driving their behaviour. To do this, you will need to seek to see their learning through their own eyes – in John Hattie's words, for the learning to become 'visible'.

It might help to tap into the solid evidence base in educational research that points in the direction of the highest quality of learning happening when learners are being appropriately stretched and in a state of 'flow'. 'Flow' is the term given by Mihaly Csikszentmihalyi to describe those moments of complete absorption that are characterised by a sense of timelessness and joy (2002). In flow states you are working at or just above the limits of your current skill or knowledge levels in a state of intensely focused motivation. You can see flow in any domain – in the intense focus of a young child creating his make-believe world, in the striving of a dancer to master a new dance, in the concentrated craft of a plasterer finishing off a wall or in the close attention given by an artist to her subject.

You may or may not recall too many flow moments from your own school memories, but hopefully you should have at least some on which to draw. The specific nature of the activity you were focused on might relate to any area of the formal curriculum or none, but it's our guess that there were at least two features in evidence: (1) you had some degree of choice in what you were doing, or the way you were doing it or with whom you were doing it; and (2) you were surprised and a little disappointed when the bell went – time flies when you're in flow.

In this chapter we will be in search of the intrinsically motivated learning focus that underpins flow. Simultaneously, we'll be outlining the thinking behind a learning-oriented route to good classroom behaviour – ie a route that transcends the punishment and reward systems of most 'behaviour management' manuals and policy documents. This isn't because these largely behaviourist approaches don't 'work' (in the sense of securing compliance) or don't sometimes have their place. It is more that they generally put the longer-term and flow-supportive goal of student-led autonomous learning well behind the quick win goal of extrinsic reinforcement and acquiescence to teacher-imposed expectations. In many cases the two goals work in direct *opposition* to each other – to the detriment of learning. This is because whereas autonomously motivated learners are focused on the *process* of learning (doing something for its intrinsic rewards), those whose motivation is controlled by others are focused on the *products* of learning (what it'll bring as a reward – be that praise, prizes or performance grades *per se*). These foci often pull in different directions.

We revisit this theme in Chapter 5 when we look specifically at the dangers of such commonplace practices as praise, stickers and merit points, but in this chapter we set out the nature of autonomy and why it is a much more precious educational virtue than compliance for learners and for teachers.

Self-determination

There are many theoretical and research-led justifications for putting autonomy at the heart of students' learning experiences. Mindset theory speaks strongly to this, but perhaps the field that addresses it most directly is that of self-determination theory, developed over many decades by Edward Deci and Richard Ryan at the University of Rochester and by other researchers across the world (Deci & Ryan 1985; Ryan & Deci 2000). Self-determination theory draws on multiple studies to posit that across all cultures there are necessary conditions for the growth and well-being of people's minds and personalities. As people, we seek these conditions out in order to meet our needs and in their absence we suffer pain and dysfunction. The conditions are:

* *autonomy* – being the perceived origin or source of one's own behaviour – not feeling like a leaf in the winds of fate and subject to others' controlling influences;

* *competence* – feeling effective in one's interactions with one's social environment and having the opportunities to express and develop one's capacities;

* *relatedness* – feeling connected to and belonging in a community with others.

Though we focus here on autonomy, in Chapter 2 we addressed the sense of developing competence through the lens of mindset, and in Chapter 6 we see how crucial genuine collaboration is to the sense of relatedness. You could do worse than see the creation of all three conditions, growth mindset, autonomy and collaboration, as being your life's work as a teacher – for every learner, in every year, for the duration of your career.

Autonomy means more than simply being able to make choices. In his influential essays on liberty, Isaiah Berlin invokes the power of metacognition in his description of the autonomous, rational self as being 'conscious of myself as a thinking, willing, active being, bearing responsibility for my choices and able to explain them by references to my own ideas and purposes' (1969, p 131). It is this powerful sense of agency and taking personal responsibility that confers the benefits of autonomy on learners.

A well-established body of research makes clear that autonomously motivated learners thrive in educational settings. *Learners* benefit when teachers support their autonomy – and so do their *teachers*: 'students achieve highly, learn conceptually, and stay in school in part because their teachers support their autonomy rather than control their behaviour' (Reeve, 2002, p 183). Here are some of the fruits of autonomous motivation, compared with learners who are motivated by their teachers' control, as synthesised from multiple studies:

- *higher academic achievement;*
- *higher perceived competence;*
- *more positive emotions about learning;*
- *higher self-worth;*
- *preference for and pleasure from optimal challenge;*
- *stronger perceptions of control (less passivity and helplessness);*
- *greater creativity;*
- *higher rates of retention.*

(Reeve, 2002, p 184)

Making it happen

With advantages of autonomy such as those set out in the previous section, two obvious questions present themselves:

- Why do teachers often practise the opposite of what learners benefit from?

- Just *how* do we infuse autonomy-supportive principles into our practice?

These two questions are clearly interrelated. Influenced by Reeve (2002, pp 191–3), we offer here a number of possible explanations for the domination of learner-control practices over learner-autonomy practices in many teachers' classrooms:

- Many teachers and teacher educators have greater familiarity with behaviour modification principles than with autonomy-generating principles: both teacher-training programmes and in-school professional development programmes tend to favour prescriptions based on sanctions and rewards rather than techniques for generating learner autonomy and personal responsibility. This is in line with the two visions of learning outlined in Chapter 1, of learning as transmission or construction. Simple, technical prescriptions override recognition that teaching and learning are complex, nuanced processes that elude quick fixes. Consider, for instance, both the superficially attractive title and the deeply contestable content of *Getting the Simple Things Right: Charlie Taylor's Behaviour Checklists*, written in 2011 by a key education adviser to the government in England.

- As teachers, it isn't always easy to judge when learners are or are not interested. So when learning isn't visible it's difficult for teachers to match their instructional decisions to the levels of interest presented by their learners. Command and control seems safer than allowing learners autonomy in their learning.

- When learners are disengaged, we often tend to resort to increasing control strategies, as it seems counter-intuitive to permit greater freedom. Consider which teachers seem to be able to provide an element of freedom for their learners and how they go about it.

- We still believe that the greater the incentive, the greater the motivation. In reality there is a 'parsimony principle' that is more effective in generating learner autonomy: what is the *smallest* incentive I need to offer in order to promote good learning? For a truly autonomously motivated learner, the external incentive is absent.

- We can underestimate learners' capacity to motivate themselves, especially if we see motivation as a fixed trait. This is in line with mindset theory: if a teacher has a fixed mindset, then if a learner's motivation is low it is tempting to use a controlling incentive to overcome the perceived deficit (rather than to seek to *grow* the learner's motivation).

- Rather worryingly, both parents and learners tend to rate 'controlling' teachers as more competent than autonomy-supportive teachers.

- Health and safety – it is possible for a teacher to convince themselves that their learners cannot be trusted to handle practical work: 'I run an autonomous classroom – she conceived the gunpowder experiment herself, M'lud.'

- We may believe that educational researchers just don't get it: '*You* try it! Autonomy in my class is a recipe for chaos/giving in/getting nothing done.'

None of these influences is insurmountable, and it's essential that we don't see autonomous classrooms as being synonymous with a laissez-faire abdication of teacher responsibility: learners are invited simply to get on with their own inquiries at their own pace – if they can be bothered to. This would be nothing like good teaching and learning. As we saw in Chapter 1, to see the process of learning as involving the co-construction of knowledge, skills, values and dispositions through experience, practice or 'being taught' is not the easy alternative to simply 'delivering' the skills or knowledge efficiently.

Especially when the task at hand is not immediately of great interest to the learner, what is far more difficult than its 'delivery' is the careful provision of big-picture rationales that explicitly link the task to the learner's sense of well-being, hopes and aspirations. This includes but goes beyond simply making the task 'relevant' to the learner: it captures again that notion identified by Berlin of bringing the learner's responsibility for his choices into rational consideration and being able to explain these by references to his own ideas, purposes, hopes and values: 'You don't see the point of doing mathematics, because your dad's offered you a job in his scaffolding firm when you turn 16? OK, so tell me Jerome about the mathematics of scaffolding – of pricing for jobs, of the geometry of standards and ledgers, of calculating the support angles required for the height of the job. Now tell me what you need to know and what you need to do to know it. How can I help you to do this yourself?'

Alongside providing a big-picture rationale to link the task to the learner's sense of self, it's important to work to develop interpersonal relationships with your learners that emphasise choice and flexibility rather than control and pressure. We know that the quality of the teacher–learner relationship plays an important role in the quality of a learner's motivation (for example, see Eccles and Midgley, 1989).

Equally important – and in many ways it supports this relationship – is to acknowledge and accept the negative feelings that some tasks might elicit: 'James, I know that you might never need to add ½ and ⅓ in your life, and to be honest outside of the classroom or examination hall I've never had to either, but for the purposes of your GCSE let's just run with it ...' This kind of complicity with the learner may be surprisingly effective, where the teacher admits that a particular topic or task is obscure, perhaps even 'boring', and needs to be tackled simply because it is in the forthcoming exam. Once accepting of the teacher's honest assessment, the learners may well settle down with a resigned shrug and enjoy the learning tasks for their own sake.

Very specifically, please note how our steer towards autonomy over compliance might impact on that tired old injunction to ensure that your lessons begin with a clear, measurable 'learning outcome' at the start of each lesson. This diktat, given life in such sexy formulations as WALT (We Are Learning To ...) and WILF (What I'm Looking For ...) fit well with the traditional, technical-rational vision of learning which sees its 'acquisition' as following relatively simple, well-ordered principles, and it can certainly have its place, for example, in helping to establish the 'big-picture' rationale described above. But do be conscious of its overuse, of its capacity to stultify, to numb the brain and to sap the life force from both teacher and learner. What is the risk that learners come to see the point of WILF-based learning being What I (the teacher, not me, the learner) Am Looking For? Have regard for research which reveals that instructional goals or objectives have an unintended and shockingly high *negative* impact on non-specified objectives ($d = -0.20$: Walberg, 1999, see Chapter 1). You can drag a learner to that lesson's intended learning outcome, but inadvertently close down any number of other, equally relevant outcomes that your learner might otherwise have reached in that lesson: a closely defined intended learning outcome impairs the learner's peripheral vision.

Allow a little space for 'alternative sexies' which speak more strongly to the constructivist vision of intrinsically motivated autonomous learners, coping richly with the detours and uncertainties en route to robust understandings:

- WWW: We Were Wondering ...

- AWOL: Another Way of Looking ...

- WISE: What I'm Still Exploring ...

- IQ: I'm Questioning ...

Finally, here's a thumbnail guide to infusing a degree of autonomy into your daily encounters with your learners. Daniel Pink (2011) calls it the 'Four Ts of Autonomy'.

1. **T**ask: Is there a degree of open-endedness about the task you set your learners? Is there scope for your learners to align it with their interests and/or areas for development?

2. **T**ime: Are there flexibilities over when the task is to be done, and when it's to be submitted?

3. **T**echnique: Does the task offer alternative routes to completion, or is there only one acceptable method?

4. **T**eam: Is this a task to be done alone, or as a team? If the latter, do your learners have any control over their collaborators?

Things to try

» Reflect on your own classroom. Consider to what extent you are developing autonomous, self-regulated learners. If you already have some level of choice for learners then consider how that might be extended. Identify a small practical step, put it into practice and evaluate its impact.

» Talk to colleagues about the development of autonomous learners. Find out what good practice is already going on in your school/department/area and ask to observe and talk to other teachers who are working to improve practice in this area.

» Take some intended learning outcomes you have used recently. Reconfigure these using some of the different suggestions above. In some forthcoming lessons, implement this different approach and reflect on whether that brings a more interesting angle to the lesson.

» Apply the 'Four Ts' to some forthcoming lessons. Make sure you set aside some time to reflect on the extent to which these had an impact on learning and learners.

» *Perhaps snatch some moments to discuss these approaches with a critical friend, share some of the suggested approaches you are working on and bounce around ideas as to how to implement these ideas, coming back to the conversation to chat about how it went.*

TEACHERS' WORKPLACE LEARNING

Becoming an inquiry-based teacher

Your work as a teacher and in your workplace will usually include reasonably high levels of accountability. You are likely to be observed in the classroom and have snapshot assessments made about your professional competence. Your longer-term effectiveness as a teacher is judged partly through your informal reputation within your school, but also by the seemingly more objective analysis of the test or examination results of your learners. Many governments internationally have become more interventionist in the curriculum and even in approaches to classroom practice. For example, the literacy and numeracy hour guidance for primary teachers in England, which held sway in the first decade of the new millennium, was very prescriptive (or at least that is how many schools and teachers interpreted it). In response to inspection regimes and external pressures, some school leaders have become increasingly managerialist, meaning that they reduce the scope for teachers' professional judgements and rely instead on prescriptive approaches and monitoring systems. The current high levels of accountability and managerialism in the education sector have been described as an 'age of measurement' (Biesta, 2011), as we have mentioned previously. The emphasis on test results, in particular, makes it all too easy to descend into a technician role, so that as a teacher you may feel you are simply 'delivering' the curriculum on behalf of the government and your school leaders. Teachers should resist this kind of descent into compliance. They should work – as very many do – individually, and particularly collaboratively, to resist this potential downgrading of their role, to retain their professional autonomy and to maintain the value placed on professional judgement.

An inquiry-based teacher

Adopting an inquiry-based approach to your work is a powerful strategy by which you will be able to develop your knowledge and expertise as a teacher and maintain your professional integrity. The interdisciplinary nature of teaching as a professional field includes elements of the subject disciplines of psychology, sociology, history and philosophy. There are also multiple paradigms within the field of education, a range of accepted but different theoretical perspectives that might be applied to any particular problem. In addition, teacher knowledge includes curriculum subject content itself, meaning knowledge of the subject(s) you are teaching. Such a complex and wide-ranging professional field means that there are different ways of knowing within the field and very little that can be simply accepted as 'good practice'. Most evidence in teaching is contested and different expert teachers and educational researchers will give you differing advice.

A typical one-year postgraduate teacher education programme is hardly likely to give you more than a brief introduction to a minimal knowledge base and a set of initial skills within this field. This is especially true because during that short training period you need to put tremendous effort into developing practical wisdom and may struggle to find time for engagement with public (published) knowledge. If you completed a three-year professional degree in teaching or a degree in education studies then arguably you will have a more substantial knowledge base. Whichever teacher education route you have completed or are completing, we would argue that you are ready to start a lifelong professional learning journey rather than holding a golden ticket stamped 'I am a good teacher'. Therefore, we encourage you to embrace the complex challenge of becoming and being an inspirational teacher:

> Teaching is not to be regarded as a static accomplishment, like riding a bicycle or keeping a ledger; it is, like all arts of high ambition, a strategy in the face of an impossible task.
>
> (Stenhouse, 1975, p 124)

This description of teaching as 'a strategy in the face of an impossible task' captures the joy of being a teacher but also its ongoing challenges. Stenhouse encourages us to continue our lifelong professional learning in the 'art' of teaching.

While a teacher must develop knowledge in curriculum subjects and in pedagogy, we support Stenhouse's argument that above all an ambitious teacher should pursue a 'mastery of seeking'. We prefer the more contemporary term 'mastery of inquiry'. For the teacher, pursuing a mastery of inquiry means developing high-level skills and dispositions of inquiry, gaining mastery of seeking an answer to the question 'What is my impact on learning and learners?'.

We strongly recommend to you this lifelong inquiry-based approach to becoming and being a teacher. You will be joining a worldwide community of teachers who have adopted 'inquiry as stance' (Cochran-Smith & Lytle, 2009). An inquiry-based approach means that an initial teacher education programme, and advanced professional education, for example, towards a masters award, should provide you with increasingly complex experiences of supporting learning, teaching, and leading learning, but require you to question your growing practical wisdom through interplay with relevant public knowledge. By 'public knowledge' we mean the published literature on learning theory, research evidence, professional guidance and educational policy.

Adopting an inquiry-based approach will help you to avoid being lost to a 'culture of compliance' that may develop in education systems that are subjected to strong central control on how to teach and what is taught, for example, by government agencies and policy (Alexander, 2010). As a developing professional you need to retain a sense of autonomy and integrity and aim to contribute to educational development in your workplace setting and more widely, rather than just passively accept the ways things are done at present.

Research that identifies key characteristics of effective continuing professional development for teachers has been usefully subjected to systematic meta-review (Cordingley, 2008; Timperley et al, 2007). The characteristics identified include:

- a clear focus on learning aligned with wider trends in policy and research;

- sustained engagement by teachers over a period of time;

- increasing ownership, collaboration and trust for participating teachers;

- classroom inquiry and experimentation;

- input of external specialist expertise or knowledge;

- collective responsibility for student learning replacing teacher autonomy;

- school leaders create conditions for professional learning and change.

The review of relevant research strongly suggests that one-off workshops and top-down training that relies on transmission of information, even if research-evidence-informed, do not provide effective professional development leading to change in practice and raised outcomes for learners. The use of inquiry-based approaches requires teachers to ask the question, 'What is my impact on learning and learners?' and then to use basic collaborative inquiry and action research methods to evaluate and develop their practice. Such an approach aims to provoke professional learning through 'interplay' between the horizontal domain of situated practical wisdom of teachers and the vertical domain of public knowledge, including published theory, research evidence, professional guidance and policy (Boyd, 2014a; Boyd and Bloxham, 2014). The role of headteachers and other school leaders is critical because they need to provide confident leadership and a workplace learning environment that encourages teachers to prioritise professional learning, allows them to question current practice and gives them space to experiment with new strategies.

Above all, Cordingley argues that 'research ... needs to be actively interpreted by users for their own context' (2008, p 49). This means, even where a substantial body of research evidence is reasonably clear and has informed national or local policy, teachers need to reconstruct, transform or mobilise that knowledge so that it makes sense for them within their own classrooms and context (Blase and Blase, 2004; Boyd 2014b; Cordingley, 2008; Levin, 2011, 2013; Nutley et al, 2008).

Informal everyday professional learning in the workplace is potentially very powerful: a school where both the teachers and the students are learning is likely to be a good or improving school. However, there are forms of informal workplace learning which can be weak because they may simply consist of imitating 'what works here' or involve weak reflection on practice leading to minor incremental change that is not evidence-based. Inquiry-based professional learning needs to align clearly with the metaphor of 'interplay' between practical wisdom and public, published knowledge.

It is important that you are proactive and adopt an inquiry-based approach yourself, but if possible this should be in collaboration with one or more allies among your colleagues. Fortunately, many schools and teachers are active in inquiry-based practice. Equally, if you do participate in a professional development programme or change project that is not explicitly inquiry-based, take charge and adopt an inquiry-based approach within that situation.

For example, you may experience the introduction of a new policy or curriculum that is presented as a compulsory change delivered through top-down information-giving sessions. With a creative, collaborative and autonomous approach you will be able to turn this kind of training into an inquiry-based approach by asking good questions, collecting data from your practice and analysing it to evaluate the impact of the changes you are making on learning and on learners. This will enable you to mediate the required changes, for example, a new policy, to maximise the positive impact on your learners.

Such a proactive style will require you to be diplomatic as well as assertive. Remember that our metaphor of professional learning as 'interplay' is useful because it acknowledges the power play involved in workplace learning contexts and relationships. But most teacher education, even the most transmissive programmes, will include some notion of 'reflection' or 'evaluation', and being particularly enthusiastic around these elements will usually provide a way in for you to develop an inquiry-based approach. If the assessment of your teaching is focused on how well you are able to mimic the prescribed 'good practice' then of course you will need to comply to a large extent and this will constrain your experimentation to some extent. But the dilemma of autonomy versus compliance applies to your professional learning! As an independent adult learner you will be able to shape your experience and your workplace at least to some extent.

The kind of power play that might constrain your professional learning may arise from national, institutional, departmental or individual influences. For example, the national system may impose a competence-based set of standards and a high-stakes inspection system that constrains teacher education at all levels to a tick-box approach. Alternatively, your school may be feeling the pressure of inspection regimes and so impose a one-size-fits-all approach to classroom teaching. At departmental level there may be a very strong set of unwritten rules within the team that sets out 'how we work here' that may tend to constrain experimentation with different teaching strategies. Finally, you may have a mentor, in a position of power over you, who has a strong and perhaps defensive set of fixed ideas about what good teaching looks like. These seemingly lower levels of constraint, because they are about interpersonal relationships, are likely to be even more powerful than national policy.

Forms of inquiry

Widely used forms of inquiry-based learning used informally by teachers as well as within more formal teacher education and development programmes include:

* **Case studies of individual learners – shadowing or supporting a learner:** This approach has the advantage of depth and of being able to empathise with the individual learner as they experience your school. Shadowing a learner for a day in your own school can be very revealing. In secondary schools, in particular, learners may move from one lesson to the next with each new setting asking them to adapt to a different teacher, a new set of behaviour rules, a particular social group of peers and a distinct subject discipline with its own language and ways of knowing.

- **Reflection in action – flexible teaching – formative assessment:** This is probably the most common and significant inquiry-based learning approach used by expert teachers on a day-to-day basis. Being flexible, changing the lesson on the spot because of the response of learners, can be a real challenge to a new teacher and you may tend to cling firmly to your carefully drafted lesson plan. Perhaps a way around that is to build formative assessment opportunities into your lesson plan and then put explicitly on your plan the instruction to yourself 'consider learner responses before proceeding'. Without getting bogged down in detail your plan might include a 'Plan B' activity in case some of the class have not grasped the key points. We know that formative assessment is a powerful driver of learning and so it is important that you focus on this and experiment (Clarke, 2014).

- **Lesson evaluation – lesson observation – assessment and feedback:** The evaluation of lessons is often a mainstay of teacher education programmes and risks becoming rather sterile and box-ticking in style. Focusing in on a particular incident, theme or piece of evidence (such as the work produced by learners) might help to enliven a lesson evaluation and add value to the process. Above all, if you try to relate what happened to some aspect of public knowledge, perhaps an idea you have come across in a professional guidance resource, then that will add value to your evaluation. Analysing video of your classroom practice is very powerful, with a camera on a tripod at the back of the room and left running, or using a well-briefed student to do the filming. Many schools will have filming permissions already in place with parents and carers, for training purposes and with set conditions for storage and use of the video.

- **Collaborative working – action learning – lesson study – action research:** Working closely with other teachers and support staff is likely to bring you the most enriching and satisfying professional development you will experience. If you get the chance to co-teach then grab it. If co-teaching is not offered to you then ask a colleague and make it happen. If you have other adults providing learning support in your classroom then be sure to include them in your planning and evaluation. Strangely, teaching can be quite an isolated profession because of the nature of the work, so make some effort to develop collaboration. In addition, take opportunities to work with teachers in other schools or with expert advisers or research mentors from other organisations. Action learning is a powerful way to work in small groups of teachers supporting each other in your work-based projects and development (McGill and Beaty, 2001). The lesson study approach involves teachers learning by collaboratively planning, observing and evaluating a specific lesson that is repeated with different student groups (Stepanek et al, 2007). Collaborative action research by teachers is a more systematic and sustained approach to inquiry and is outlined in Chapter 5.

- **Critical friend – student voice – formal mentor – line manager:** Identify critical friends who can help to guide your professional learning. Find a colleague whom you trust and ask them to be your informal mentor. Consider your learners as critical friends and use their evaluative feedback to guide your development as a teacher.

The way that you go about this will depend on your context, but remember that you need to analyse the student voice rather than just accept it at face value. You will need to show response to student evaluative feedback, otherwise your learners will become cynical. Your response might be to explain why 'it is not possible to watch movies *every* afternoon ... but as it happens this afternoon we will be watching a short clip from ...'.

- **Analysis of grades – formal appraisal – observation by an inspector:** This type of inquiry is more formal, sometimes out of your direct control and possibly a little bit scary. It is helpful to maintain an inquiry-based approach even in these more formal kinds of appraisals. Try to maintain a questioning approach to the process and to any feedback you are given. Of course, power will be a significant element of your working relationships with line managers and external inspectors and you will no doubt be willing to sacrifice an element of autonomy in order to keep your job or gain your teaching qualification. However, in the education business the priority is generally learning and learners. If you are able to demonstrate a focus on learning and back up your arguments by showing careful analysis of data, then you will find most managers and inspectors are impressed and willing to be persuaded. As a professional teacher you should assert your right to contribute to knowledge and to the wider profession.

- **Formal programmes:** Completing a formal practitioner-research-based masters programme for teachers will provide you with a firm base for leading inquiry-based projects and enable you to lead change in practice in school. Completing a masters is a sound and suitable formal qualification on which to build your career as an educator. In many countries teaching is a masters-level profession. Some teachers enjoy their masters so much that they go to the extreme of pursuing a professional doctorate. We would argue that the commitment required to complete a part-time doctorate means that you must have personal as well as professional reasons for pursuing this, or have an ambition to move to an academic or research role.

Sources of data

This list of types of inquiry-based learning includes several sources of data, including: observation and classroom video clips; being observed and being given feedback; questioning and other formative assessment; student work; student grades; student voice; and feedback from other teachers as your collaborators or mentors. From this list we would particularly pick out the work that your learners produce. This work provides rich data that are likely to be more meaningful and nuanced than grades and closer to the learning. If you are able to see evidence of progress in the work your learners produce, that is good evidence of learning. Some of the data will already be available within the classroom or school but some will require systematic collection. It is the critical, rigorous and systematic analysis of this range of data that will help you to draw reliable conclusions from your workplace learning. It is important to analyse and interpret the data rather than just describe and accept what they seem to show at face value.

This need for analysis is particularly important with 'student voice' data where learners have been asked for evaluative feedback. After teaching a series of lessons on a topic, the student feedback may be overwhelmingly positive: 'I feel I now really understand the topic'; 'the lessons really helped to explain everything'; 'the teacher made everything really clear'. First you might question the truthfulness of the responses. More importantly, you might feel that the learners may have been spoon-fed and insufficiently challenged.

Perhaps even more contentious is the need to question grade data. For example, a team of teachers introduce a revised approach to their teaching and wish to evaluate its impact. Surely, if the learners have achieved high grades then that is good evidence to support the use of the teaching strategy? First, this may become quite technical, using predicted grades and value added, using base line and post-testing or using comparative performance of the learners in other subject area texts or exams. If you wish to calculate effect size, a useful measure of the difference between pre- and post-test results that helps to evaluate the impact of an intervention on a group of students compared to a control group, then you need to be sure that the test you use is reliable. In some ways, however, the bigger issue is to consider the research question carefully. The key question, 'What is my impact on learning and learners?', goes beyond just the grade achieved and asks how that learner has been developed and prepared for their next challenge.

Developing an inquiry question

While you may have a generally questioning approach to your work you should consider sometimes pursuing more systematic in-depth inquiry into a key issue you are facing at present. What will be the focus of your inquiry? How will you decide among the numerous possibilities? In the busy world of a teacher there is a justifiable emphasis on immediacy and so a tendency to focus on evaluating interactions, learning activities and lessons. The high level of accountability will create pressure to focus on school priorities, the requirements of external inspectors and on raising test or examination results.

We suggest five considerations that in combination will help you to develop ambitious systematic inquiry projects and to refine the inquiry question which needs to be at the heart of your investigation:

- **Consider impact:** Use this key question as a starting point for inquiry: What is my impact on learning *and* on the learner? Whatever issue or situation you choose to focus on, by including a focus on the learner this question will help to avoid over-reliance on simplistic measures of educational achievement or progress.

- **Bottom-up – top-down:** Try to identify an inquiry question that links bottom-up issues and top-down policy drivers from school leaders, inspectors and policy. What issue or dilemma have you noticed in your own classroom or department and how does that relate to national or institutional policy? This will help you to question the influence of your wider context on practice and on student learning.

- **Stakeholders:** Consider the different stakeholders involved in an issue. Perhaps start with learners but widen your gaze to include others involved, including teachers, parents, teaching assistants, school leaders, inspectors, employers and the wider community. As well as helping to position your inquiry in a wider context this will also help you to identify the power relationships and ethics involved.

- **Interplay:** Consider how your issue involves both practical wisdom and public knowledge. What ways of working in your school are involved? What relevant body of public knowledge, theory, research evidence, professional guidance or policy is available and what does it tell you about the issue? Engagement with public knowledge will help to refine your inquiry question but remember that your context is particular and so you should ask of public knowledge, 'What does this mean for me, my learners and my school?'

- **Data:** Consider what sources of data are relevant to your issue. This may include the learners' perspectives, the work they produce and the grades and feedback they have received from teachers. Asking in a very concrete way, 'What data are available and how will I collect and analyse them?' will help you to refine your inquiry question and design to make it ambitious but practicable.

Characteristics of teacher inquiry

Teacher autonomy versus teacher compliance. This dilemma applies just as much to you as a teacher as it does to your learners. Consider how inquiring you are, how you might develop a questioning disposition as a teacher, because this will help you to retain professional autonomy. Consider how questioning you are, and might become, about public, published knowledge, such as this book. Also consider the value you place on practical wisdom, ways of working in your school and classroom; consider avoiding uncritical acceptance of these ways of working, even if they are well established. Consider how questioning you might be about local, regional and national policy, including any prescribed curriculum; do not uncritically accept these because they are published by the government. In implementing policy continually ask the question: 'What is my impact on learning and learners?'

You will have come across the concept of teacher learning through 'reflection'. Unfortunately, reflection has often been used in weakly defined ways and that has undermined its value. We support forms of critical, reflective learning, but recommend a language of 'inquiry' because it helps to emphasise the need to pursue systematic investigation into your practice, based on data collection and analysis in relation to external public knowledge.

Teacher inquiry may operate at different levels in terms of time and scope. In the very short term you might respond within a lesson to how learners are engaging with the lesson and change your plan immediately. This kind of flexible teaching is a high-level skill that requires confident handling and a set of alternative strategies to hand. As a beginner, this is not always easy. It is worth remembering to empathise with the learners, for example, by explaining why you are amending the planned activity. You may feel that being open and vulnerable in this way is too risky and will reveal you as a novice, but actually your ploughing on with a failing strategy is far more likely to be regarded with disdain by learners. Explaining the need to change direction will allow you a period of grace to bring the class back together, perhaps review progress and then give some instruction on what is to be done next. It is important to build your own programmes of inquiry that are more long term than such changes within individual lessons. We would recommend that you identify a theme for inquiry, an issue that is bothering you, and investigate it over the medium term, perhaps through a sequence of lessons or a unit of work.

As one element of an inquiry-based approach it may be helpful for you to think about your lesson planning. Rather than thinking in a sequence of Plan – Teach – Assess, it can be helpful to switch this around and think of it as Assess – Plan – Teach. Assessment helps you know what your learners know and can do at present, and of course this is a good starting point for planning a challenging lesson or sequence of learning activities. An inquiry-based approach means following through multiple cycles of Assess – Plan – Teach, but identifying issues that concern you, critically engaging with public knowledge, and using systematic analysis of data to investigate the question 'What is my impact on learning and learners?'

Things to try

»   *Identify a problematic teaching, learning or assessment issue in your classroom and focus on evaluating it within a specific lesson or during a morning session. Identify at least two ways of collecting and analysing relevant data and try to tease out a change in practice you might need to experiment with.*

»   *Identify an issue and use a simple method to gather and analyse the student 'voice' in your classroom. Depending on your inclination and the age of your learners you might ask them to 'Draw a picture/cartoon/doodle/image to show how you feel about today's maths lesson' or 'Write non-stop for two minutes about what you found most interesting and most difficult in science today.'*

»   *Select an issue in your practice that deserves a sustained inquiry over a sequence of lessons or days. Find and critically engage with some relevant public, published knowledge, perhaps a professional development book or online resource. Pursue data collection and analysis to investigate your practice and evaluate any changes that you decide to make. Identify a critical friend and discuss your findings to help you decide on next steps or a new line of inquiry.*

Reflections on Humza's mathematics lesson

Before going further you might wish to reread Humza's mathematics lesson set out at the start of this chapter and reflect on it in the light of the ideas discussed in the 'learning power' and 'teachers' workplace learning' sections above. How does Humza's lesson connect to the dilemma 'autonomy versus compliance'?

Here are some thoughts from us, but remember that you will bring your own ideas to the issues arising and much depends on the context of your work in a particular school and classroom.

1. Do you think Humza is being too hard on himself? What are the positive features of the lessons?

Humza is fortunate to be working with a teacher mentor who values this sort of creative, real-world approach, though it is perhaps understandable that as a beginning teacher, Humza feels less confident. Sometimes, however, we find that we take negative comments to heart more than we do positive ones, so it is the colleague's comment about noise level which shakes Humza's confidence (even though this may have been a very off-the-cuff comment). There may be some teachers who do not welcome experimentation, and prefer to play it safe, but Humza needs to prioritise collaboration with the teacher whose practice seems more positive – he may be able to learn a lot from closer collaboration with this colleague. The idea that a noisy lesson equals a poor lesson is quite an outmoded one, and even though this view may linger on in some quarters, Humza needs to be confident that the noise level in itself is not a sign of a lack of learning (it may be true on occasion, but is far from being a given).

In relation to autonomy, Humza's authentic mathematics is providing plenty of opportunities for choices by the students and for them to gain ownership of the learning. Who will they work with in the survey, what data will they collect, what features of the phone do they value, what kinds of graph will they choose to use, how will they hard-sell their contract? Having framed the mathematics problem, Humza is allowing the students to take some control. Even if one or two of them need some coaxing to keep focused, at least Humza has most of the class getting on with the activity while he does some monitoring and works with individuals or small groups.

It is important that Humza does not feel he has to wait to adopt such strategies as he does here, or feel as though he has to master 'basic' practice before he takes risks. Seeing himself as an autonomous learner from the outset and promoting autonomous learning among his students are not things he has to wait to do, so there are many positive features on which he can focus here, while retaining appropriate critical reflection.

2. What do you feel about the level of noise in a classroom; how does it relate to learning?

Looking on the bright side, the lesson may have included more talk about mathematics than Humza thinks. Reflecting more carefully on his own observations during the lesson, asking the teaching assistant for a perspective and checking the children's work might provide useful evidence on this. Talking around the mathematics problems, listening to the ideas of others, providing feedback and teaching each other all align with a constructivist learning approach so that noise, a reasonable level of noise, might be a sign of focused active learning. Autonomy means the learner develops responsibility and self-awareness by adopting the 'plan, do, reflect' cycle of the self-regulated learner (Zimmerman, 2002). 'Planning' independently means setting goals and adopting strategies to achieve them. 'Doing' independently means monitoring your own progress, shaping the environment to support your progress and managing time effectively. It seems unlikely that such practical planning and doing activity could be achieved effectively without at least some lively discussion to gain feedback from peers. Humza might consider developing routines for individual, paired and small-group work that have associated rules around noise levels. It is also possible to coach learners to use 'close-up' voice levels, to imagine that the person they are talking to is holding their hand! There are plenty of strategies to promote and manage group work, and many schools are keen to support such practice.

3. **How do you feel about Humza's intended learning outcomes and what impact might they have on learning and learners? How open-ended are the learning outcomes that you use in your lesson planning?**

The sequence of lessons planned by Humza is based on a fairly open-ended task and seems to present a high level of challenge for the students. Within the overall challenge of hard-selling a phone contract through creative work on an advert, there are smaller achievements possible along the way, such as calculating a mean or constructing an accurate graph. While it may be useful to consider carefully the learning outcomes for the particular lesson, it also seems useful for the students to keep in mind their overall purpose in the project. Having very open-ended outcomes on the whiteboard, but then negotiating success criteria with the class, for example, around accuracy and choice of graph, might be a more useful way forward in this situation. For example, surely having a WALT of 'present data to hard-sell the contract' is likely to be more meaningful and motivating than Humza's choice of 'presenting different kinds of data'.

Humza might find it useful to experiment with alternative ways of sharing the purpose and learning outcomes of lessons, although he will need to work within the spirit of the school's approach or negotiate permission to go beyond this. Most importantly, there seems to be a gap between the practical activities in the lessons and the key concepts in the mathematical ideas that underpin the topic. Rather than worrying too much about presenting the learning outcomes, this could be tackled using carefully planned key questions that Humza might interject at suitable moments within the inquiry and in the plenary to each lesson to help the students step back and see the big picture. This is something we will explore further in Chapter 4.

4. **Humza seems pretty certain the learning outcomes were not met in lesson two. How do you think Humza might change the lesson if he had the opportunity to teach it again?**

It is initially tempting to suggest that Humza structures the activities more carefully, for example, by creating a data-collection sheet for the survey. However, this might lead the lesson to become increasingly framed by the teacher and with less choice and control by the students. This approach may be necessary in a situation where classroom control is challenging. An alternative might be for Humza to do some reading on the management of group work. Organising the class into small groups and providing some ground rules for collaborative working may be one way to provide structure in this lesson without reducing autonomy.

5. **Did Humza make a good decision to risk this authentic mathematics approach? Why not simply use worksheets with different examples of data and have students get plenty of practice in the data-handling tasks?**

Importantly, *really* understanding a mathematical concept seems far more likely where the data are meaningful to students' lives. Working down multiple examples on a worksheet is likely to teach students in a more mechanical way, but if the data mean less to them then it may not lead to deep understanding. Humza's attempt to engage the students with authentic mathematics seems very worthwhile. He has seen over-reliance on worksheets in a previous placement, so he seems to know deep down that his approach is more likely to succeed, plus he is working with a colleague who seems to share this view. It seems as though it is more of a confidence issue for Humza – he does not need convincing of the worth of this approach, but he may need convincing that he is capable of teaching this lesson well. Fair enough, he might need to make the students more familiar with his way of working so that they follow routine rules and he can keep their discussions at a more reasonable volume. Teaching them to imagine the person they are talking to is on their phone, only an arm's length away, is a useful way to capture this. By building a lesson around a problem that is authentic for the learners, meaning it has value for them in the real world outside of school, the teacher is already likely to increase engagement. Learners will recognise the problem and bring some existing knowledge to it. This will increase their sense of belonging. There is an issue of social justice involved here because if the teacher can make the classroom activities more authentic for all of the learners, for at least some of the time, then school may become less of an alien experience for learners from disadvantaged backgrounds.

6. **To what extent should Humza relax about this individual lesson which may have not gone quite according to plan? As one lesson within a sequence, is it possible for him to see it in a more positive light?**

Reflecting as an independent learner means self-evaluating your methods, analysing the causes of success and failure and identifying strategies for future success. This applies to Humza in relation to his learning as a teacher. Humza's sequence of lessons looks like a good use of time overall and even his noisy lesson on its own meets the 'four Ts' of autonomy: Task, Time, Technique and Team. The task is open-ended, the time is flexible, the techniques are varied and teamwork is required. Clearly, there is room for development and Humza needs to consider to what extent he is nurturing autonomy. An effective teacher develops self-regulated learners by setting high expectations, creating structured opportunities for learners to practise planning their work, allowing them to work independently while monitoring their own progress and by requiring them to self-assess their work and reflect back on the process of learning.

There is plenty of opportunity for Humza to develop his own autonomy here, by learning more about these approaches, by collaborating with his colleague, by reading more blogs, teaching resources and research evidence that will inform his view. Humza does not currently know how much deep learning has gone on in this lesson because he is too concerned about surface issues. Once he gets beyond this, he will be able to interrogate more meaningfully what has taken place in this lesson and be in a stronger position from which to reflect on future work.

Things to try

» *Adjust the planning of one of your lessons to address the 'four Ts' of autonomy: Task open-ended; Time flexible; Techniques varied with different possible routes to success; Teamwork required. Gather and analyse everyday data (observation, learner voice, teacher assessment of work produced) to evaluate the impact on learning and learners.*

Chapter 3 summary

This chapter has focused on the dilemma 'autonomy versus compliance'. This dilemma creates cognitive dissonance for many teachers because the pressure on curriculum delivery, external inspection and test results seems to favour creating compliant learners in closely controlled classrooms with teacher technicians 'delivering' the curriculum.

Learning power

- Autonomy as a learner means achieving a level of self-awareness and taking responsibility for considered decisions.

- Learners are seeking autonomy, competence and relatedness, and as a teacher it is your responsibility to create a learning environment that satisfies this.

- Behaviourist approaches to managing the classroom may have a part to play in establishing clear boundaries but could be in tension with the development of self-motivated independent learners.

Teachers' workplace learning

- If you are to grow as a teacher and make a full professional contribution then you should consider adopting an inquiry stance towards knowledge and practice in your field. This means questioning all aspects of practical wisdom and public knowledge and daring to challenge powerful influences and well-established traditions.

- Day-to-day reflection is important but you also need to engage in more systematic, sustained and focused inquiry that leads to collaboration with colleagues, draws on public knowledge and analyses available data such as the student voice, student work, teachers' written feedback and student grades.

- Inquiry-based professional learning requires an element of classroom coaching (observation and feedback), both as a source of data but also as an encouragement to embed change in practice, so direct observation by a colleague or use of video (which might be made by a learner) are crucial tools for inquiry.

Taking it further

- In designing learning activities that build autonomy, consider open-ended Tasks, flexible Time, a range of possible Techniques and some element of individual control within Teamwork. Read further on developing a metacognition 'wrapper' around a learning activity; for example, consider the additional readings on 'metacognition and self-regulation' in the EEF's *Teaching and Learning Toolkit*, available at: http://educationendowmentfoundation.org.uk/toolkit/meta-cognitive-and-self-regulation-strategies/.

* You might establish inquiry-based learning as a teacher, seeing learning through the eyes of your learners, as a routine element of your work. There are many good action research websites and books for teachers, and we suggest Baumfield et al (2013) as an accessible, thoughtful and practical guide.

* This useful paper on supporting autonomy by Johnmarshall Reeve is available open source online: *Teachers as Facilitators: What Autonomy-Supportive Teachers Do and Why Their Students Benefit*. It is worth reflecting on your current practice and considering how small changes might help you to move to a more 'autonomy-supportive' approach. Available at http://sdtheory.s3.amazonaws.com/SDT/documents/2006_Reeve_TeachersAsFacilitators.pdf.

References

Alexander, R. et al (eds) (2010) *Children, Their World, Their Education: Final Report and Recommendations of the Cambridge Primary Review*. New York: Routledge.

Baumfield, V., Hall, E. and Wall, K. (2013) *Action Research in Education* (2nd edn). London: Sage.

Berlin, I. (1969) *Four Essays on Liberty*. Oxford: Oxford University Press.

Biesta, G. J. J. (2011) *Good Education in an Age of Measurement: Ethics, Politics, Democracy*. Boulder, CO: Paradigm.

Blase, J. and Blase, J. (2004). *Handbook of Instructional Leadership: How Successful Principals Promote Teaching and Learning* (2nd edn). Thousand Oaks, CA: Corwin Press.

Boyd, P. (2014a) Learning Teaching in School. In H. Cooper (ed.) *Professional Studies in Primary Education* (2nd edn). London: Sage, pp 267–88. Companion website available at: www.uk.sagepub.com/upm-data/61142_Cooper.pdf (accessed 1 May 2015).

Boyd, P. (2014b) Learning Conversations: Teacher Researchers Evaluating Dialogic Strategies in Early Years Settings. *International Journal of Early Years Education*, 22(4), pp 441–56.

Boyd, P. and Bloxham, S. (2014) A Situative Metaphor for Teacher Learning: The Case of University Tutors Learning to Grade Student Coursework. *British Educational Research Journal*, 40(2), pp 337–52.

Boyle, B. and Charles, M. (2014) *Formative Assessment for Teaching and Learning*. London: Sage.

Clarke, S. (2014) *Outstanding Formative Assessment: Culture and Practice*. London: Hodder.

Cochran-Smith, M. and Lytle, S. L. (2009). *Inquiry as Stance: Practitioner Research for the Next Generation*. New York: Teachers College Press.

Cordingley, P. (2008) Research and Evidence-Informed Practice: Focusing on Practice and Practitioners. *Cambridge Journal of Education*, 38(1), pp 37–52.

Csikszentmihalyi, M. (2002) *Flow: The Psychology of Happiness. The Classic Work on How to Achieve Happiness*. London: Random House.

Deci, E. L. and Ryan, R. M. (1985). *Intrinsic motivation and self-determination in human behavior*. New York: Plenum.

Eccles, J. and Midgley, C. (1989) Stage–Environment Fit: Developmentally Appropriate Classrooms for Young Adolescents. In C. Ames and R. Ames (eds) *Research on Motivation in Education*, vol. 3, *Goals and Cognitions*. New York: Academic Press, pp 139–86.

Kemmis, S. (2006) Participatory Action Research and the Public Sphere. *Educational Action Research*, 14(4), pp 459–76.

Levin, B. (2011) Theory, Research and Practice in Mobilizing Research Knowledge in Education. *London Review of Education*, 9(1), pp 15–26.

Levin, B. (2013) To Know Is Not Enough: Research Knowledge and Its Use. *Review of Education*, 1(1), pp 2–31.

McGill, I. and Beaty, L. (2001) *Action Learning: A Guide for Professional, Management and Educational Development* (2nd edn). London: Kogan Page.

Nutley, S., Jung, T. and Walter, I. (2008) The Many Forms of Research-Informed Practice: A Framework for Mapping Diversity. *Cambridge Journal of Education*, 38(1), pp 53–71.

Pink, D. (2011) *Drive: The Surprising Truth about What Motivates Us*. New York: Riverhead Books.

Reeve, J. (2002) Self-Determination Theory Applied to Educational Settings. In E. L. Deci and R. M. Ryan (eds) *Handbook of Self-Determination Research*. Rochester, NY: University of Rochester Press, pp 183–203.

Ryan, R. M. and Deci, E. L. (2000). Self-determination theory and the facilitation of intrinsic motivation, social development, and well-being *American Psychologist* 55, pp 68–78.

SEDL (2002) Getting to the Heart of the (Subject) Matter. *Classroom Compass*, September 2002. Available at: www.sedl.org/pubs/classroom-compass/cc_v5n3.pdf (accessed April 2015).

Stenhouse, L. (1975) *An Introduction to Curriculum Research and Development*. London: Heinemann.

Stepanek, J., Appel, G., Leong, M., Mangan, M. T. and Mitchell, M. (2007) *Lesson Study: A Practical Guide for Teachers and Facilitators*. London: Sage.

Taylor, C. (2011) *Getting the Simple Things Right: Charlie Taylor's Behaviour Checklists*. London: Department for Education. Available at: www.gov.uk/government/uploads/system/uploads/attachment_data/file/283997/charlie_taylor_checklist.pdf (accessed 26 August 2014).

Timperley, H., Wilson, A., Barrar, H. and Fung, I. (2007) *Teacher Professional Learning and Development: Best Evidence Synthesis Iteration*. Auckland: New Zealand Ministry of Education.

Walberg, H. J. (1999) Productive Teaching. In H. C. Waxman and H. J. Walberg (eds) *New Directions for Teaching Practice and Research*. Berkeley, CA: McCutchan, pp 75–104.

Zimmerman, B. J. (2002) Self-Regulated Learning: An Overview. *Theory into Practice*, 41(2), pp 64–70.

Chapter 4 Abstract versus concrete

This chapter is about

* engaging with the 'big' ideas that underpin lessons and learning;
* developing 'meta-learning' and 'metacognition' in the classroom;
* the knowledge teachers need, including pedagogy and curriculum subject content.

Introduction

Abstract versus concrete? Don't good teachers and good writers back up their explanations by using concrete examples to illustrate more abstract concepts? Surely learners need some basic factual knowledge in order to solve problems? When does 'abstract' prove to be better for learning that being more down to earth and 'concrete'?

We consider that highlighting the dilemma 'abstract versus concrete' helps teachers to avoid too much focus on the detailed subject 'content' of a lesson or sequence of lessons. We are not denying the importance of content, but rather suggesting that by starting to plan with a focus on the concrete, it is possible to lose track of the key concepts, the more abstract big ideas within the curriculum subject discipline that underpin the lesson or activity.

Learners need to approach and engage with an abstract concept through practical problem-solving activity. However, a key challenge for the teacher is to ensure that coverage of content does not become the sole purpose of the lesson. After all, Howard Gardner (1991) memorably warns us that coverage is the enemy of understanding. Equally, we would warn against approaches that over-emphasise 'learning to learn' in the absence of meaningful content knowledge. The teacher's role is to orchestrate a balance between engagement with a key concept within a curriculum subject and the development of thinking dispositions. The teacher then asks our key question: 'What is my impact on learning and on learners?'

In this chapter we focus on the learning power of 'meta-learning' (focusing on the key concepts within a curriculum subject discipline) and of 'metacognition' (reflecting on the process of learning). In relation to teachers' workplace learning we focus on what 'knowledge' or 'knowing' teachers need, for example, to be able to plan sequences of powerful learning activities. In this chapter we will argue that 'abstract beats concrete', meaning that as a teacher you need to facilitate meta-learning for your learners and you need to plan learning activities in relation to the relevant key concepts within curriculum subjects.

CLASSROOM SCENARIO

David's geography lesson

We had been studying our topic for three weeks: the Vikings and their settlement across large areas of Britain around a thousand years ago. My class was full of enthusiasm after our whole-school day trip to visit a Viking museum. I had planned to capitalise on the experience of the trip by moving on, in the following week, to a whole-class role-play activity. There were loads of ideas on the web about Viking role-play lessons, and I borrowed and adapted them to design a challenging activity that would involve an element of cross-curricular, creative learning.

My initial idea was that we would think about why the Viking settlers chose the sites they did to build their villages. When I say this was my idea, what I mean is that this was my interpretation of a classic lesson that has been developed and adapted by geography teachers over the years to suit their purpose and local context. I divided the class of 30 into six different specialist groups, to represent the opinions of woodcutters, water carriers, farmers, soldiers and thatchers (who need reeds to build and repair thatched roofs). I provided a simplified map of the area and each group had to debate where they would want to build their settlement and why, according to the varied needs of the villagers. I then reorganised the class into final decision-making community groups. These new groupings each had one woodcutter, one water carrier, one farmer and so on. As intended, this led to huge debates as each community group had to resolve different opinions and reach a decision on where they would build their settlement. The debate centred on the different needs of being close to forest, a water source, land for growing crops and grazing animals, an easily defended position and a marshland where reeds for thatching could be harvested. High-achieving children within the class were given an additional challenge in relation to 'chairing' a group discussion, and prompt cards for each role supported the expectation that all learners would contribute to the discussions. Each group had to present their proposal to the rest of the class and we would vote. I got swept up in the idea, and so did the class.

My headteacher asks teachers to submit half-termly plans showing intended learning outcomes, a basic structure for each lesson, resources and cross-curricular links. When it came to filling out that box for cross-curricular links it seemed obvious that this would be a spoken language activity, which was useful because I hadn't recorded an assessment for that area of learning for a while. I also thought we could measure distances from the sites chosen for the settlement to other locations, for example, to the river for water and the forest for firewood, and that would contribute to our work in mathematics. My main intended learning outcome for the session was: 'We will begin to understand why the Vikings built their settlement in that particular place.'

The children loved the lesson, and I got a real buzz from it. Each group was totally on task, thinking of their own reasons for choosing a particular location, and the bit when each group presented was fantastic; I thought their arguments showed real understanding of their knowledge of the Vikings. I went home feeling pretty good about it all, but then two things happened that have knocked my confidence in the value of the lesson.

On my way to school the next day, I popped into the local shop to pick up a sandwich for lunch. The mum of one of the boys in my class served me. They're building a new enormous supermarket just over the road from school and there's a campaign for people to keep using the little local shops, so I try to support it when I can, as it's quite a tight-knit community around the school. At first I was delighted she mentioned the lesson and how much he'd enjoyed it, but as I walked out of the shop, I replayed her words in my head 'George is loving your lessons on the Vikings, he didn't shut up yesterday about how much he enjoyed being a Viking farmer.' This niggled at me a bit, but I wasn't exactly sure why. Then, after I'd done the register and we were moving on to writing up an account of the previous day's lesson, I asked my usual question, 'What did we learn about in yesterday's lesson?' Most of the hands went up, I asked five people and got five versions of the same sort of response: 'We learnt about the Vikings', or if pushed, 'We learnt about why the Vikings built their village on the hill above the river.' I asked them to think about it again, talk to a partner and think if there was anything else that they learnt, and I got a few more tentative responses: 'We learnt about how far it was from the river to the village'; 'We learnt about how the Vikings might have spoken to each other.'

Their enthusiasm was still undimmed, and we went ahead with the writing exercise. But I went home that day feeling less pleased with myself. Yes, they had learnt even more about the Vikings and their villages. But was this really the point of my lesson? I no longer felt so sure. As I left the school entrance I carefully drove my car around the road works caused by the building of the main entrance to the new superstore. It occurred to me that it was a silly place to put a superstore. I thought about the corner shop run by my student's family and realised they must be worried about the effect on their business, and I wondered if the lesson was really about where things get built and who decides. Or maybe the lesson was about how communities and groups of people work together or against each other, how tensions are resolved in human interaction. Above all, I was worried that the children saw absolutely no connection whatsoever between the 'then' of the lesson and the 'now' of their lives.

Questions about David's lesson

1. What was this lesson about? What was David really trying to teach in this lesson? What was it the children were supposed to be able to do or understand?

2. What did the children seem to make of the lesson? In what way is the issue of the new supermarket relevant to the lesson?

3. What steps could the teacher take if they were teaching this lesson again, to engage learners with the big ideas underpinning the lesson?

4. What are the implications of this case for the way teachers engage with national curriculum documents and develop school-level schemes of work as well as individual lessons?

5. What are the implications of this case for your approach to developing your own subject-discipline knowledge as a teacher?

LEARNING POWER

The learning power of going 'meta'

Ask a learner what sort of thinking they needed to do to solve a problem and you've asked them to engage in metacognition. Metacognition can be defined as thinking about thinking (or 'knowing about knowing'), and therefore involves a regulative element – getting 'above' or 'beyond' the activity to reflect on the thinking process itself and how one can do that more effectively. Similarly, metacognition's close cousin meta-learning involves learning about learning. Both processes can be elicited when you ask children questions like 'What kind of thinking are you doing here?', 'Have you done anything like this before?' and 'Why do you think this task is so hard?'

Meta-learning and metacognition are deeply connected to both the content and the processes of learning. So a good deal of learning to learn operates within curriculum subject disciplines and involves the learner's engagement with key concepts, the 'big ideas' within the subject content that underpin learning activities, case studies and examples introduced by the teacher or discovered by the inquiring learner. Meta-learning therefore includes learners' engagement with epistemology, the 'ways of knowing' within specific curriculum subject disciplines. Getting to grips with these ways of knowing helps a learner to 'become' a mathematician, a historian, a geographer and so on. For example, understanding a scientific method through the design of an experiment is fundamental to becoming a scientist.

Both metacognition and meta-learning are high-order skills which enable the learner actively to monitor and regulate their progress, as well described by the actor Tobey Maguire (Spider-Man!): 'I'm self-aware enough to understand that it's statistically very hard to achieve the position I'm in, but … I find the way, like water; I like to be productive. I'm constantly reflecting on personal progress. I got those ideas aged 15, and they've been north stars to me' (Tobey Maguire, 'I Always Knew I'd Be Successful', *Guardian*, 11 May 2013). It is interesting that Tobey can locate so specifically the time he discovered the power of going meta – could there have been an inspirational teacher involved?

This book represents an invitation to meta-learning in the professional field of teaching, but we made a particular feature of this in the learning power section of Chapter 1 when we asked you to reflect on your understanding of two contrasting metaphors for learning – learning as *acquisition* and learning as *construction*. When you are asked to get above the concrete particulars (of a lesson plan, for instance) into the heady, higher-order altitude of abstraction (what type of learning might be happening here?), certain demands are made and they're not always comfortable. But they are essential at the top end of learning, both for teachers and their learners.

When researchers examine vast numbers of studies of the most powerful influences on academic achievement (known as 'meta-reviews' of research), there is one consistent finding: regular engagement in robust metacognitive and meta-learning activities raises the achievement of learners. One such researcher, Robert Marzano, describes metacognition as the 'engine' of learning. In a range of different approaches used internationally, metacognition and meta-learning are often described in such terms as 'self-regulation' or 'deep reflection'. Little wonder that one of these researchers, John Hattie, insists that the teacher's job is not to make learning easy – it's to make it difficult. It's in these difficult-to-reach territories that learners are forced to stretch beyond their existing skills and knowledge in order to construct links and conduits to new skills and new knowledge. This is at the heart of constructivist learning – using existing knowledge to (co)construct new knowledge with the aid of a skilled facilitator of learning – asking the right questions, probing for inconsistencies and exceptions and challenging thinking. In the poet Robert Browning's memorable expression, we should allow our reach to exceed our grasp, or what's a heaven for?

Evidence for going meta

Let's explore some of the evidence base for the power of abstraction, as revealed by the great synthesisers of research studies:

- There is strong evidence from research meta-reviews on the impact of regularly getting learners to identify similarities and differences – mental operations which require the learner to 'get above' the concrete particulars to see the ways in which two or more elements are alike or different (Marzano et al, 2001). This example of meta-learning has claimed effect sizes from 0.88 to 1.76 – equivalent to shifting a learner's performance from 50 per cent to 81 per cent or more.

- The learning power of metacognitive strategies for supporting learners to get 'above' the content in order to engage with abstract conceptual principles is claimed by Margaret Wang (Wang, Haertal and Walberg, 1993). A more recent research meta-review has found such metacognitive strategies to lead to achievement gains of eight-plus months (*d* = 0.67) and that this approach represents *high impact at low cost* (Higgins et al, 2011).

- In another meta-review, significant metacognitive elements, often in the form of self-regulation processes, were one of the highest-ranking influences on raising achievement (Hattie, 2009). In addition, Hattie cites research suggesting that 'When tasks are very complex for the learner, the quality of metacognitive skills rather than intellectual ability is the main determinant of learning outcomes.' This is because in conditions of high challenge, learners can't rely on their existing data-sets of skills and knowledge – they must improvise, and improvisation encourages learners to exercise higher-order skills, to think about their thinking.

Implicit in Hattie's observation about complex tasks is the call to ensure a healthy diet of challenging tasks for every learner. Only in the *absence* of challenge and complexity does intellectual ability become a strong determinant of learning outcomes. So if you do find a close correlation between your learners' cognitive test scores and their learning outcomes and a weak correlation between their metacognitive skills and their learning outcomes, be just a little concerned: this might point more to an impoverished learning environment than to the predictive power of intellectual ability.

In a newspaper article the sports psychologist Kerry Spackman provided a high-profile example of metacognitive skills trumping ability in situations of high challenge. Explaining the reasons for the Formula 1 star Lewis Hamilton's success he responded to the suggestion that Hamilton was simply born with the ability to go fast by arguing, "What he has is what Schumacher had – a structure and a process for how to learn and improve. Every experience is a learning experience. It wasn't a load of random things happening to him. Lewis is the same – he obviously has talent, but he's a vastly superior driver now because he's learnt how to learn, which most drivers don't do. Every experience has a way of being analysed, understood and filed away. He doesn't just pound around a race-track repeating the same old habits"' ('The Brain Rewiring and Supercharging That Makes Hamilton a Master', *Guardian*, 26 May 2007). Spackman is arguing that Hamilton did not merely learn about aspects of racing cars, he also learned to learn. So rather than learning, for example, about how to manage the wear and tear on his tyres during a race, Hamilton learned how to learn about managing the tyres and kept right on learning.

Note how this issue around high-challenge tasks sits uneasily with the dominant 'acquisition' vision of learning, which aspires to the mechanical simplicity of efficient knowledge transfer, and a possible explanation for the high status that 'ability', streaming and setting are given in this vision.

As a teacher you might initially consider the underpinning key concept behind every lesson you plan: this is a much better starting point than mere content or learning activities that have 'worked' before. Having identified the key concept(s) that learners will engage with during the lesson, you will begin to identify possible learning activities and detailed content, but always with an eye on your aims in relation to the impact both on learning and on learners. You will need to consider what issues the learners will explore, what questions they will ask, what skills and dispositions they may develop and how you will allow them a degree of autonomy in the way that they tackle the tasks.

Getting 'above' the concrete

To move from the meta-review of research data to one practical instance of the power of abstraction – getting 'above' the concrete particulars – consider an adaptation of a study first conducted in the 1940s (Duncker, 1945). Two later researchers (Gick and Holyoak, 1980, p 307) drew on the initial idea in their own experiment and in so doing demonstrated the power of analogy:

> *Suppose you are a doctor faced with a patient who has a malignant tumour in his stomach. It is impossible to operate on the patient, but unless the tumour is destroyed the patient will die. There is a kind of ray that can be used to destroy the tumour. But if the rays reach the tumour all at once and at sufficiently high intensity, the healthy tissue that the rays pass through on the way to the tumour will also be destroyed. At lower intensities the rays are harmless to both healthy tissue and the tumour. What type of procedure might be used to destroy the tumour with the rays and, at the same time, avoid destroying the healthy tissue?*

Only 10 per cent of people solved this problem. When this problem was followed by another story, however, the success rate rocketed to 90 per cent (based on Gick and Holyoak, 1980, p 309). See if you can figure out why:

> *A small country was ruled from a strong fortress by a dictator. The fortress was situated in the middle of the country, surrounded by farms and villages. Many roads led to the fortress through the countryside. A rebel general vowed to capture the fortress. He knew that an attack by his entire army would be sufficient to capture the fortress, so he gathered his army at the head of one of the roads, ready to launch a full-scale attack. However, the general then learned that the dictator had planted mines on each of the approach roads. They were set so that small bodies of soldiers could pass over them safely, as the dictator himself needed to transfer his troops and workers to and from the fortress. A larger force, however, would detonate the mines. It seemed impossible to capture the fortress, until the general hatched a plan: he divided his army into small groups and dispatched each group to the head of a different road. At an appointed signal, each group marched down a different road to the fortress, arriving at the same time, and capturing the fortress.*

What seems to happen is that once the clear connections are made between the second story and the first intractable problem, the solution becomes obvious. The story had its own solution embedded within it, of course, and we needed simply to abstract the core idea (attacking the 'enemy' from multiple directions, each direction being of low strength but collectively amounting to great strength) and transport it into the initial problem. This skill of analogy, importing ideas from one domain into another, perhaps wildly different domain, is excited by the opportunity to think metacognitively – what is the big idea here? Can we borrow something from one area that might be useful in another? Can we make useful *connections*? Classroom implication: encourage learners to identify central characteristics and thereby to get 'above' the material from an analogous perspective.

Moving beyond learning to learn within curriculum subject disciplines, Howard Gardner identified the power of connection-making in a short interview in *The Psychologist* magazine in October 2003: 'Interdisciplinary thinkers are able to draw on a variety of methods and concepts in order to approach and solve problems that cannot adequately be resolved through traditional practices drawn from a single discipline.' As a teacher, you will do well to encourage the skills of connection-making in your learners. Some learners will seem to do this of their own accord, like Alice Bell, Science Policy Research Unit Research Fellow at the University of Sussex: 'I finished A levels barely bothering with formal chemistry exams but boasting a final fine art piece inspired by hydrogen bonding, English lit coursework exploring fictionalised physics, and having studied a history syllabus largely devoted to nuclear proliferation. I've hardly looked back since' (Bell, 2013).

But all learners will benefit from your explicit and regular invitations to go 'meta'. This account from a secondary English teacher, Chris Reck, was given to one of the authors some years ago:

> Hi Barry – Just to let you know that I have started using some of the thinking strategies you recommended, and they have been particularly successful, for instance cross-curricular links relating learning from previous lessons to learning objectives. I remember you said that the idea behind this was to demonstrate how to make connections – ie the teacher demonstrating the thinking process. Here's an interesting one. I am teaching Of Mice and Men as a different cultures text. In particular we are examining the idea of the American Dream. I asked my class to tell me what their previous lesson was and their learning. Half had come from Food/Tech and half from Design/Tech. The learning? You can only freeze food if it is below 5 degrees C, the conditions that cause metal to rust, and how to make a kebab. Connections to the American Dream? Well, Lennie and George want to have a place of their own so they have the freedom to choose who they can invite round and share what they have produced from 'the fatta the land' – could well be a kebab that they'd kept frozen. Metal rusts? Rust is a form of corruption/death: an interesting metaphor for the erosion of our dreams. This was particularly powerful. By the time we had read Chapter 4 we were able to discuss the 'rusted dreams' of several of the characters. Another example was a group who had been studying the rise of Hitler in History earlier that day. They themselves made the connection to the American dream – Hitler persecuted the Jews, homosexuals etc. in order to realize his vision of the perfect society. Only connect!

Chris was a fairly newly qualified teacher at the time, but he went on to become an exceptional Advanced Skills practitioner who regularly invited his learners to make abstract connections, creating an extensive set of connection-making activities for this purpose.

The metacognitive domain isn't the preserve of secondary teachers, despite some misinterpretation of Piaget's work that certain high-order cognitive functions must necessarily await the teenage years. From the early years onwards, you can get children to make connections between apparently unrelated objects ('How is this the same as this? How are they different?'), to compare, to contrast, to classify, to make and to deconstruct analogies and metaphors, to become proficient in and to exercise strategic judgement in the use of graphic organisers like comparison matrices ('Compare and Contrast'), Plus Minus Interesting (PMI) matrices, Venn diagrams, Diamond 9 ranking rubrics, thinking maps and the like. These are all different ways of providing a visual scaffold to material. For instance, Diamond 9 rankings require the learner to rank nine elements from most to least important:

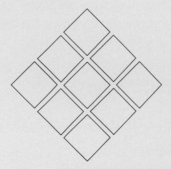

We close this section of the chapter by inviting you to make connections with the previous chapter. There we cited Berlin's conception of 'freedom to' being underpinned by a consciousness 'of myself as a thinking, willing, active being, bearing responsibility for my choices and able to explain them by references to my own ideas and purposes' (Berlin, 1969, p 131). Demand for yourself and for your learners the right to exercise agency over your life and learning and theirs. Take responsibility for your choices and get them to take responsibility for theirs. And to explain them – go meta.

Things to try

» *Search online for a clip of the comedian Father Guido Sarducci's 'Five Minute University' and reflect on what this has to say about the balance between the concrete and the abstract in contemporary education!*

» *Introduce the concept of 'going meta' to your class, and use the term as often as possible. Seek out opportunities for the class to 'get above' the concrete particulars of a lesson to the guiding principles by asking questions with a meta-dimension: What's the big idea in this question? What type of question is this? Have you done anything like this before? What's the tough bit in this task and why is it tough?*

» *Invite your class to ask meta-questions and write these up on the board/flip chart as they emerge, acknowledging their value and significance.*

» Consider a lesson you are currently planning. Work on your intended learning outcomes for the lesson. Ask yourself about the underpinning concept(s) of the lesson and consider how your learners will demonstrate their increased understanding. Consider key questions and other strategies for making connections between the 'concrete' facts and examples that the learning activities involve and the more 'abstract' bigger picture of the underpinning concept. How will you use explicit strategies for meta-learning?

» Similarly, think about the metacognitive aspects of your lesson. Identify thinking dispositions such as curiosity, persistence, creativity, logical thinking, collaboration or independent learning that might be particularly useful to learners in this lesson. Create opportunities within the lesson, even if it is just part of the plenary, for learners to reflect on the process of learning, for example, by considering the question: 'What learner skills have I used and how did they help me to tackle the task?'

TEACHERS' WORKPLACE LEARNING

Teachers' pedagogical content knowledge

What does an effective teacher need to know? This question has been debated for many years and is still a highly contested issue. A key issue is how the skilful teacher combines knowledge of how to teach (meaning instruction or pedagogy) with knowledge of what to teach, the curriculum subject content (meaning, for example, a key concept or skill in mathematics). If you have studied a traditional subject discipline, at advanced level in school or college and especially as a first degree, then to some extent you will have developed a strand of identity, for example, as a 'historian', 'mathematician' or 'scientist'. Now as a beginning teacher you will be engaging with new knowledge on how to teach, and this pedagogical or instructional theory (sometimes referred to as 'didactics') will have challenged some of your existing 'common-sense' ideas about what makes a good teacher. In Chapter 2 we talked about teacher identity, to what extent you see your identity as first and foremost 'teacher' or first and foremost 'geographer' or 'scientist' or 'mathematician'. You may wish to consider how these are connected, whether your identity is a 'teacher of geography' or a 'teacher of science'. And are you leading your learners to become scientists, geographers, historians ...?

If you are a primary class teacher then you may need to develop a wide range of content knowledge across the curriculum subjects, including a confident grasp of literacy and numeracy. If you are a subject specialist teacher you need in-depth content knowledge in your particular subject discipline, but you also need knowledge of literacy and numeracy. There is a real debate about the importance of different kinds of teacher content knowledge. Certainly many people, when fondly recalling their school days, will claim that their own passion for a particular subject was initiated primarily because of the passion of a particular teacher for that subject. A professor of geography at Liverpool University (Andy Plater) secured relatively poor geography O- and A-level grades but went on to achieve eminence in his field. When asked what had inspired him to study geography at university in the face of mediocre results, he identified two inspirational geography teachers who had faith in him and who revealed to him the excitements and possibilities of geography beyond the formal and examination-bounded curriculum.

From a sociocultural perspective (Blackler, 1995) we would argue that the professional knowledge or 'knowing' of a teacher is usefully seen as having five characteristics:

- teacher knowledge is dynamic – you will be continually learning;
- teacher knowledge is situated – your school context will shape what you learn;
- teacher knowledge is social – you will develop your knowledge within a team;
- teacher knowledge is contested – there is debate on what and how to teach;
- teacher knowledge is mediated – it is shaped by language, rules (including unwritten rules), key ideas and values within your school as a workplace and within society;
- professional knowledge is an element of teacher identity.

So what are the implications of this dynamic, situated, social, contested, mediated and identity perspective on teacher *knowing*?

First, you cannot expect to learn everything you need to know at the start of your teaching career. This applies equally to how to teach and what to teach. Professional standards and teacher training supervisors may at times seem to expect this, but you need to be realistic and not try to be superhuman. You will need to prioritise your learning and accept that you will only gradually develop expertise as a teacher. The key here is to build your inquiry-based teacher learning strategies so that you do continue to develop throughout your career. Consider yourself as a self-regulated learner in relation to becoming an inspirational teacher. Use meta-learning and metacognition strategies to develop your own professional learning.

Second, the complexity of becoming a teacher may at times seem overwhelming and no doubt you will tend to focus on practical wisdom and want to gather 'tips for teachers' that you can immediately try in your classroom. But despite that understandable urgency, you need to remember the 'interplay' metaphor and seek to draw on public knowledge to help to evaluate the learning activities and approaches you gather. Kurt Lewin, the inventor of action research, famously stated that 'there is nothing so practical as a good theory' (1951). You might consider that there is often nothing so invisible as a good theory, meaning that much learning theory becomes common sense and is viewed by teachers as practical wisdom. To draw out this underlying theory you might reflect on the assumptions underpinning the practical tips you are offered by experienced colleagues. Teachers working in other schools or even just departments in the same school are also an important resource to help you to stand back and question the local practice and ways of working in which you are becoming embedded.

Pedagogical content knowledge

Teacher knowing includes knowledge of how to teach (pedagogy) and combines this with knowledge of the curriculum subject content (for example, of science, history or mathematics). As a teacher, you need to bring together these different areas of knowledge to inform your practice in planning, teaching and assessment. An influential body of work on this process has been completed by Lee Shulman and his colleagues at Stanford University. One key idea was the overlap of areas of knowledge to form the 'pedagogical content knowledge' of a teacher as illustrated in Figure 4.1.

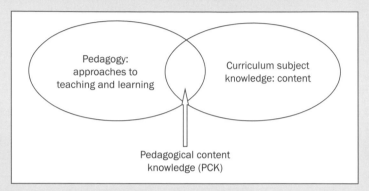

Figure 4.1 *A teacher's pedagogical content knowledge (PCK)*

Within Figure 4.1 the curriculum subject content knowledge means the key ideas, ways of knowing and skills of a subject discipline such as history, science or mathematics. The pedagogy or approaches to teaching and learning means knowledge of how children learn and strategies for planning, inclusion, facilitation and assessment. Where these two overlap represents the idea developed by Lee Shulman of 'pedagogical content knowledge', which is referred to as PCK. Pedagogical content knowledge may be defined as the teacher's understanding of key concepts in the subject discipline and how to teach them effectively, including the most powerful explanations, demonstrations, metaphors and concrete examples to make the key concepts, skills and ways of knowing within the subject discipline accessible for learners (Shulman, 1986). 'Location' is a key concept in geography, illustrated, for example, by the 'least-cost' location in terms of transporting the raw materials to a factory. This idea of 'location' is the key concept or big idea that underpins David's lesson in the scenario at the beginning of this chapter. As a teacher David is perhaps too focused on the detailed content of the lesson, which seems to be about Vikings and settlements, rather than on this key concept of 'location'. Note that two other concepts might also be approached in that lesson. The concept of 'time' is addressed in the sense that the landscape reflects decisions made in the past, and the concept of 'decision-making' is addressed in the sense that location decisions are influenced by environmental, economic, social and political factors.

Implications of PCK

First, whenever you are planning a lesson or sequence of learning, you need to focus initially on key concepts and only then will you need to identify concrete examples, case studies and learning resources. In practice this will often work the other way around, but still you must identify the key concept or big idea underpinning the purpose of the lesson. You need to appreciate that your teaching and professional learning will be strongly situated, meaning that it will be shaped by ideas, rules and objects that seem commonplace and taken for granted in your school workplace. For example, a 'scheme of work' or the school's idea of 'excellent work' or the resources available for a particular topic will affect your decisions and approaches. Your understanding of a key concept within a curriculum subject will shape your approach to teaching the lesson, but so will the view of how to teach that concept held by your teaching team or mentor teacher. A useful way to focus on pedagogical content knowledge is to step back from the planning or evaluation of a lesson and ask: 'What are the big ideas or key concepts within the subject, underpinning the purpose of this lesson?' This understanding of key concepts within curriculum subjects is not something you are likely to master solely through individual study, although that will be a part of the process. Discussion and collaborative planning of lessons and medium-term schemes with other teachers will be a key opportunity for professional learning.

Second, you should be aware that teachers who are learning new curriculum subject content may have a tendency to resort to teacher-led and content-heavy lessons. This is understandable: there is so much new information and a teacher-led lesson in some ways may seem less risky. While not suggesting that you can afford to be unprepared, we propose that if you are willing to risk using inquiry-based learning for your learners then one benefit is that you can position yourself as a learner and model being a learner within the subject discipline. So in preparing lessons try to focus on your understanding of the big ideas, the key concepts, and derive some key questions related to those, rather than trying to learn all there is to know on the topic. Design learning activities based on a constructivist approach that are active for the learners, making them do the hard work. Consider to what extent you might be able to develop more challenging and open-ended learning activities using learners' current and background knowledge, supplemented by their research using resources such as text books, other learners, the local community and, if available, the internet. Remember the mantra 'no risk, no learning'.

The wider context

Pedagogical content knowledge is not set in stone and does not exist in a vacuum. What is taught in classrooms and how it is taught are heavily influenced by the wider context of schooling, community and educational policy frameworks. For example, in your school what is considered to be the school science subject of 'biology' may be affected by the level of subject expertise within the teaching staff, the geography of the local area and wider region and relevant national curriculum policy or guidance set by regional or national government. The influence of the local community and economic activity is likely to at least influence the choice of case studies used in lessons, for example, related to local types of farming, manufacturing industry or other commercial activity. The regional or national curriculum guidance or wider culture is likely to influence the position of biology as a science subject in its own right, alongside, for example, physics and chemistry, or as a part of a broader concept of combined 'science'. In this way, 'school biology' is different from the wider conception of the subject discipline and has its own characteristics and content. It is therefore helpful to

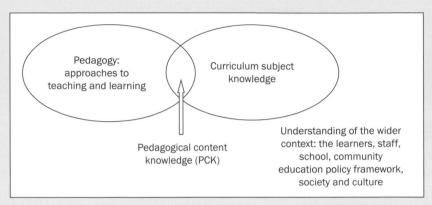

Figure 4.2 *A teacher's pedagogical content knowledge within the wider sociocultural context*

place Figure 4.1 into a box representing knowledge of the local community and the wider educational policy framework.

By including the wider context, Figure 4.2 acknowledges the power that schools and teachers hold as they mediate the influence of the community and of educational policy. It is important that you maintain a reflective awareness of the beliefs and values that you bring to the role of teacher. For example, local community or national values around diversity issues may sometimes appear to clash with your moral and professional responsibility to support *all* of your learners. Whatever your personal and political beliefs, a teacher has a moral obligation to support all of their learners in an equitable way and to set themselves high professional standards in creating an inclusive classroom and school.

So what are the implications of considering teachers' knowledge within this wider context?

First, and most importantly, you will want to know your learners in order to build effective working relationships with them and to empathise with their experience of schooling. This is an absolute priority and involves practical steps such as:

- knowing names;
- greeting learners on arrival at school and at each lesson;
- meeting and talking to them outside the classroom;
- checking their records, including learning needs and previous school reports;
- working with learners in extra-curricular activities.

This priority placed on knowing your learners includes, as far as possible, getting to know their parents and their wider community. You need to be able to empathise with your learners and as far as possible understand their viewpoint on school and education. This reflection on the relational aspect of teaching is developed further in Chapter 6, but before you move on from this paragraph just pause for a moment and imagine yourself as a parent or carer. In terms of priorities for schooling, knowing that your child is really known and talked to as a unique individual on a day-to-day basis is sure to be high on your priorities, if not at the top of them.

Second, you will be aiming to build links from the wider context into your classroom. This includes illustrating key concepts within the subject discipline by using relevant examples and case studies in lessons that learners will recognise from their local community and economy. It also means giving learners choice and control to select topics for inquiry from the wider world that interest them. You may also be able to bring experts in from the local economy or use visits to engage with local social and economic activities. These approaches force you to engage with and get to know the local community and will help to make you more empathetic and genuine to your learners.

Third, you will try to question regional or national curriculum policy and mediate the way that it is interpreted into schemes of work and lessons for your learners. As a professional you must not simply accept national or regional policy on the school curriculum: that would position you as a technician 'delivering' prescribed schooling. Instead, you must question, interpret and mediate the curriculum to suit your learners within their local context and support them in their wider education.

Fourth, you will not wish to ignore the big picture of your role in developing beliefs and values within the community and wider society. Schooling is a huge intervention by a society into social, cultural and economic development, and it is essential that you question its impact on your learners. Being a teacher is a privileged position in society with considerable autonomy, at least at classroom and school levels, to influence young people. It carries with it big responsibilities in terms of nurturing beliefs and values in children and young people. You will want to continue to read, reflect and think about your impact on learners through shaping their education as members of society and global citizens. You will want to reflect on your own values and behaviours because you will be a role model for children and young people.

Teacher identity and practice

A final amendment to the model of teacher knowing is required. Learning teaching involves 'being' and 'doing' as well as 'knowing'. Your practice and identity as a teacher is part of the mix and overlaps with your knowing of pedagogy and of curriculum subject content. In Figure 4.3 we have added 'identity and practice' in order to acknowledge their importance in shaping the knowing of a teacher (see Chapter 2). This creates an overlapping 'hot spot' where PCK is aligned with teacher identity and practice. We propose this diagram as a model of teacher knowing and argue that this hot spot represents those lessons or teaching moments when 'flow' is achieved so that your practice as a teacher is completely focused on the learning of your learners. These are the moments when your teacher knowing is flowing and you may achieve the status and impact of an inspirational teacher. We introduced flow in Chapter 3 in relation to children's learning, but now we will consider it briefly in relation to your learning as a teacher.

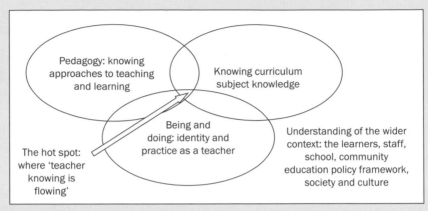

Figure 4.3 *A teacher's knowledge, identity and practice in context – giving the possibility of 'flow'*

The concept of flow, developed by Mihaly Csikszentmihalyi, has most often been applied to sport or other skilled activities such as playing an instrument. Flow is 'the way people describe their state of mind when consciousness is harmoniously ordered, and they want to pursue whatever they are doing for its own sake' (2002, p 6).

It is possible to consider the classroom teacher as comparable to a participant in an extreme sport, such as a rock-climber, because of the unfortunate and potentially dramatic effects of failure in both situations. Teaching, or rock-climbing, at the limit of your ability requires a kind of concentration that is focused rather than stressful, that is calm rather than nervous and that is more akin to a relaxed flow than a concentrated effort. Flow means not self-consciously managing your performance but still operating at a high level near the edge of your current ability. Teacher flow means classroom teaching that is well planned and yet flexibly responsive to children's engagement and learning, that hits the hot spot where different forms of teacher knowing come together and that might seem like hard work but will also be deeply satisfying.

As a beginning teacher, first you need to be realistic – you must not expect to experience 'flow' in your teaching every day. However, you are likely to achieve flow for occasional short periods, and when you do then you should enjoy it, reflect on it and use teacher inquiry tools to consider how you can work towards making it happen more frequently.

Second, it is important that you consider your professional learning as 'interplay' between vertical public knowledge and horizontal practical wisdom as discussed in Chapter 1. Take care not to over-rely on practical wisdom, but equally do not dismiss local ways of working too easily when considering research evidence or policy. Seek to inform your teaching and build pedagogical content knowledge through engagement with public knowledge, including learning theory, research evidence, professional guidance and policy.

Third, whatever formal and informal professional learning activities you engage in, it is important that you embed your new thinking or knowledge through practical activity. You might use an advanced-level textbook to consolidate your understanding of a key concept within a curriculum subject, you may have the opportunity to observe another teacher or you may attend a professional development workshop. All of these activities are likely to remain isolated and relatively ineffective unless you use some of what you have learned to make a change in your classroom and use inquiry to evaluate its impact. This enactment is an essential element of teacher learning.

Things to try

» *Consider your current professional development targets and what actions you are taking to address them. Consider to what extent these target areas include some focus on developing your curriculum subject knowledge. Make this as practical as possible, draw up a learning 'to do' list. Your list might include issues to explore using books and websites, teaching strategies to explore and experiment with, great teachers you will observe, critical friends you will meet with to debate issues, teacher networks you will join and contribute to. Make sure some of this list is focused on developing your curriculum subject knowledge as well as your pedagogical skills.*

» *Think about your best lessons and sequences of lessons when you have experienced 'flow' in your classroom. Reflect on this to identify what contributed to this successful event and take practical steps to experiment in your classroom and make it happen more often.*

Reflections on David's geography lesson

1. **What was this lesson about? What was David really trying to teach in this lesson? What was it the children were supposed to be able to do or understand?**

'Geography is maps' provides a concise definition for the subject discipline. Geography is about understanding spatial patterns and the particulars of place, asking how a particular place became as it is today. David was teaching a modified version of a classic decision-making lesson focused on location, location, location! As a teacher you need to have sufficient grasp of the subject discipline(s) you are teaching so that you are able to recognise the key concepts underlying particular topics, case studies and examples. You need to be able to analyse the lessons that you inherit when you join a teaching team or school and are working with a scheme of work produced by others. David needs to have subject knowledge about the Viking context (concrete) but also needs to have a good grasp of the underpinning concepts in geography of location and of decision-making in society (abstract).

The lesson as it stands engages learners with economic aspects of location by considering transport costs. This may be referred to as seeking the 'least-cost' or 'prime' location. The lesson also engages children in the social aspects of location by considering the different views of the villagers. It somewhat innocently assumes that all the settlers will have an equal say in choosing the location. Small changes to the lesson details could be made to introduce environmental and political aspects of location, but arguably these might make it too complex. The key issue for consideration here is whether the desired learning for the lesson is limited to understanding something about Viking Britain, or whether there are bigger questions to ask: a greater 'sense of place'. These questions are about location of particular settlements and settlement patterns but even more abstractly about location decisions that help to explain the landscape. The concrete knowledge in the lesson is about Viking settlements, but the more abstract concept is about 'least-cost' location in geography, as well as being about social interaction and competing perspectives.

David unfortunately failed to really engage his learners with these bigger, more abstract, ideas, and therefore, despite facilitating a busy and active classroom, he missed the opportunity to enable his learners to approach a key concept within the subject discipline. If his routine planning and teaching included a metacognitive element then this may have helped him and his learners to reflect on the wider purposes of the lesson. Using hinge questions after each stage of the activity, and in a substantial plenary at the end of the topic, meta-learning in this case would have helped to develop a focus on the two key concepts of prime location and of decision-making in society. This is when the location of the new supermarket becomes a powerful example and connects the lesson more clearly to the learners' experiences. Adding a well-developed meta-learning plenary may have moved David's lesson from effective to inspirational.

2.   What did the children seem to make of the lesson? In what way is the issue of the new supermarket relevant to the lesson?

The children understandably focused on the concrete example used in the lesson and on the whole did not 'get' the big ideas of least-cost location and the social or political processes by which such decisions are made. The possible building of a new supermarket in the local area would form a perfect extension or parallel to the lesson because it is a location decision that is tangible, local and relevant to the children's lives. It highlights the economic, and especially the political, aspects of location decisions. Relevance is a hot topic in education, and we often read that learners find it helpful if learning is relevant to their lives. In encouraging the children to compare the Viking settlement activity to a contemporary supermarket planning application, the relevance comes through them seeing that geographical patterns develop over time. They then come to realise that the purpose of the lesson is about the key concept of 'location' rather than being about the detailed content of the history of Viking settlements.

However, we must not overlook the fact that the children really enjoyed this lesson and were fully engaged in the process, to the extent that some of them had obviously talked about it at home. David had fired their imaginations. The children had also, it seems, co-operated with each other really well, working in groups and engaging in discussion. We are certainly not denying that some learning took place. What we are saying is that there could be another layer or two to the learning, one looking at the abstract concepts and the other encouraging some reflection on the learning process itself. In fact, these approaches could be fed in relatively easily and this would take the learning to a new level.

3. What steps could the teacher take if they were teaching this lesson again to engage children with the big ideas underpinning the lesson?

The lesson might be run in pretty much the same way but perhaps combining a concrete learning outcome (to understand how the location of the Viking village may have been decided) with a more ambitious and more abstract learning outcome (to understand how humans make decisions and affect the patterns in our landscape). It is also possible to consider a learning outcome related to skill (to listen and speak within a group to reach agreement on a decision). Learning outcomes addressing abstract concepts need careful wording and would need further explanation during the lesson. The teacher should prepare a hinge question, one that the whole lesson turns upon, and that focuses on the abstract concept(s). This hinge question could be used half-way through the lesson and in the plenary and in this case might be: who and what has affected where things are found within the landscape?

As an alternative to presenting well-thought-out learning outcomes at the start of the lesson, it might be better to turn this on its head and interrupt the lesson half-way through and ask the children to come up with the learning outcomes. We might also consider whether the use of intended learning outcomes often tends to make us focus on more concrete outcomes and lose sight of the more abstract concepts and purposes of the lesson.

4. What are the implications of this case for the way teachers engage with national curriculum documents and develop school-level schemes of work as well as individual lessons?

In England a national curriculum has existed in various forms since 1988. New governments often fiddle with it in a centralised way that has direct implications for teachers' planning and therefore for children's learning. However, there is a complementary danger that some schools and teachers may interpret the curriculum guidance in a very direct and burdensome way and end up with stodgy schemes of work that are heavy with content.

Even if the curriculum guidance you have to consider as a teacher is content-based you might be able to step back and ask: 'Why was this piece of content chosen?' For example, in England the curriculum might include studying the 'Tudors' as an important period of history. But the reasons for studying the Tudors are not so that every child in England has some idea of who Henry VIII was or that he was a colourful character. The reasons for studying the Tudors is surely at least in part about the big ideas that are illustrated by investigating this period, including the role of religion and of the monarchy in the British government. In science the curriculum may include study of the alkali metals and partly this is because of the potential for dramatic explosive experiments such as putting potassium or magnesium into water. But more importantly, the alkali metals conveniently demonstrate the patterned relationship between atomic structure and reactivity.

Now some teachers may argue at this point that learners cannot cope with big ideas until they have learned the 'basics'. This is an attractive idea that might conveniently justify a relatively straightforward diet of teacher-led 'chalk and talk' lessons relying on transmission. But we know from innovative work such as Philosophy for Children (eg Hymer and Sutcliffe, 2012) that even very young children can engage with big ideas such as the meaning of life or the concept of infinity. Lawrence Stenhouse uses learning to play chess as a simple model of learning within a subject discipline. He argues that an objectives-led approach may be useful for teaching the very basic moves, but to learn beyond that the teacher may merely advise on principles and help the learner to evaluate successes and failures. He suggests that teachers need to celebrate when the learner moves beyond their level of knowledge and beats them at chess (1975, p 37). We need to repeat the point emphasised by John Hattie: the teacher's job is not to make learning easy – it's to make it difficult. Approaching big ideas within the curriculum subject disciplines challenges learners and requires them to construct new ways of thinking about the world.

In the two examples from history and science it is important to note that the ways of thinking within those subject disciplines are as important as the key concepts. Young children should experience historical investigation and scientific experimentation and take early steps in 'becoming' a historian and a scientist. As Stenhouse points out, 'the superficialities of the disciplines may be taught by pure instruction, but the capacity to think within the disciplines can only be taught by inquiry'. Within an inquiry-based approach, 'one can think in a discipline at elementary as well as advanced levels of study' (1975, p 38).

If David were to consider a holistic view of supporting his learners as 'thinking like geographers', then this may help him see beyond the immediate confines of the lesson. Curriculum subject disciplines will of course usually include 'concrete' topics and there will be information and facts which need to be learned. However, we should expect children to handle factual content (concrete) at the same time as thinking more conceptually. Historians are often asked, 'If you had a time machine, where would you travel to?' and in a surprising response the historian Sam Willis's answer was 'to the future' (BBC, 2015). He argued that like all good historians he is interested in the effect of the past on the future, and he sees this as the most exciting thing about his work. We can apply this not only to David's geography lesson, but to any lesson where we are looking at historical contexts or artefacts. We and can keep our eye on the fact that learning is at its most exciting when learners make connections between 'then' and 'now' and see the relevance of particular issues to their own lives or to the lives of others. We've pointed out that people may argue that this comes later: first you learn concrete facts, then later you are able to make wider connections. We would argue that this approach does not need to be withheld until high school, college or university, but that engaging with abstract concepts can be part of learning from a much younger age.

Overall then, a teacher such as David, depending on their particular workplace setting, might adopt some combination of the following strategies when interpreting curriculum documents and planning schemes of work or individual lessons. Above all, it is important that teachers use their autonomy and creativity. They might:

•   Step back from detailed content and consider how this lesson or series of lessons might really challenge the learners and stretch their thinking to approach some of the key concepts underpinning the subject discipline.

- If you are working with curriculum guidance documents that seem heavy on detailed content then check carefully the introduction and guidance sections. Sometimes curriculum guidance is interpreted by teachers or headteachers in a rigid and content-heavy way that was never the intention of the authors of the documents. Try to identify the big ideas or key concepts underpinning the design of the curriculum. Consider why some topics are included and others left out.

- Reflect on your personal beliefs around the level of abstraction and the big ideas in subject disciplines with which learners can meaningfully engage. If you are a teacher who believes in the need to 'cover the basics' before studying key concepts, then take a look at projects such as Philosophy for Children or even good-quality documentary television programmes aimed at children.

- Consider how your personal subject knowledge is affecting your chosen strategies. For example, where we have limited knowledge, we may tend to resort to teacher-led approaches, because these give more control and avoid questions from learners to which we do not know the answer.

We are not suggesting that you should reject or ignore the national, regional or institutional guidance on curriculum in your school setting. What we are suggesting is that you take control of it, working within your teaching teams, and interpret it wisely for the benefit of your learners. The main strategy we have proposed is to identify the key concepts and ways of knowing and to design learning activities that engage your learners with these key ideas and the skills required to 'become' a member of the subject discipline. Collaborate with other teachers in this work because you cannot expect to have really well-developed curriculum subject-discipline knowledge early in your career, especially if you are a primary teacher teaching across a range of subjects.

5. What are the implications of this case for your approach to developing your own subject-discipline knowledge as a teacher?

Always seek out and find out more about the big idea or key concept that is at the heart of the content 'covered' by your lessons. Seek out connections between your own subject specialism or interest and the lessons you are teaching, try to push forward your own learning of each curriculum subject discipline. Your subject-discipline knowledge should also develop by engaging with items in the news that touch upon the curriculum subject disciplines you are teaching. At the local, national and international level this is a great way to identify authentic problems and relate them back to key concepts and skills in the subject disciplines. By monitoring and searching online you will find multimedia resources available to use in your classroom.

Second, this case highlights the importance of building meta-learning into your teaching routines. This meta-learning should focus on the key concept underpinning the content of the lesson as well as on the process of learning. Provide opportunities for the learners to reflect on what they have learned and how they have learned it. Encourage learners to identify and explore the abstract concepts, to ask questions themselves, to make connections, rather than delivering a set of concrete learning outcomes and then gaining agreement at the end that they have been met. Encourage them also to reflect on the process of learning during the lesson(s), considering what thinking skills they have applied and developed. Consider how planning in detail for a complex lesson, including the practical preparation of resources, might tend to keep us so busy as a teacher that we fail to see the wood for the trees. Planning needs to be as much about thinking as it is about practical preparation if we are to be ambitious as teachers.

Third, at a further level of metacognition for you as a teacher, you might usefully reflect on the dispositions that your lesson design and facilitation may be nurturing within your learners. A disposition is a tendency towards a particular intellectual behaviour. It means not only having a skill but being inclined to employ that skill by habit in your thinking and learning. Consider to what extent your lesson design and teaching may be influencing the thinking dispositions of your learners, for example, their learning habits of persistence, being questioning, working collaboratively, thinking logically or thinking creatively.

Things to try

» *You might develop your approach to planning by engaging selectively with an existing scheme and focusing on dispositions such as: setting high goals; managing distractions; curiosity; persistence; logical and creative thinking; collaborative and independent working; and reflection (Costa and Kallick, 2014; Lucas et al, 2013).*

» *Consider of one class you teach in order to connect abstract concepts in the curriculum to students' lives. Think through the different layers of knowledge you have about the class that influence your relationship with them and your plans for their learning. Start with the individual learners – names, their lives outside school, the way they interact with each other – consider gaps in your knowledge and how you will learn more. Next, think about your knowledge of the local community and consider how you might learn more and make connections in your lessons. Finally, consider your learners as global citizens and consider how you might develop their capacity to investigate, empathise, communicate and take action in relation to world issues (Mansilla and Jackson, 2011).*

Chapter 4 summary

This chapter has focused on the dilemma 'abstract versus concrete'. This dilemma creates cognitive dissonance for many teachers because we know that providing concrete examples is a key strategy in teacher explanations, and case studies and practical tasks are essential for engaging active learning.

Learning power

• Tackling challenging, complex tasks in your classroom, tasks that are also perhaps interdisciplinary, leads your learners beyond dependence on existing skills and knowledge so that they are forced to improvise and begin learning to learn.

- Metacognition involves reflecting on your own thinking and is an element of becoming a self-regulated learner. In the debriefing following a challenging task, time is well spent asking the question 'How did we learn?' and reflecting on the dispositions required for success.

- Meta-learning involves learners in stepping back from detailed content to consider the underlying key concepts that they have been approaching. Planned teacher questions and the plenary should challenge the learners to consider 'What did we learn?'

Teachers' workplace learning

- In planning lessons and sequences of lessons, you should focus primarily on key concepts within the curriculum subject – think 'location' rather than Viking settlement (de Echevarria and Patience, 2008)! If you are instructed to 'deliver' an existing programme, then work backwards to identify the underlying key concepts and mediate the set materials and activities as required.

- In planning your professional learning of the curriculum content, it is helpful to think of teacher knowledge as including pedagogy (how to teach) and curriculum subject knowledge (what subject content to teach). Where these two areas of knowledge overlap is called pedagogical content knowledge (how to teach a particular subject effectively).

- It is helpful to think of a sweet spot in your classroom teaching that occurs when your practice and identity overlap with pedagogical content knowledge. You are concentrating without concentrating and the challenge is high and the learning is good and life is good and you are in flow – if it has happened once, then you know it is possible again!

Taking it further

- Developing the emphasis on meta-learning and metacognition in your classroom will help you to raise your expectations and will encourage your learners to embrace challenge and accept failure and mistakes as opportunities for learning. Find out more and start to experiment with changes in your classroom practice that help your learners to become self-regulated learners: consider the Teachers' Pocketbook on *Teaching Thinking* for accessible further guidance. If you have access to an academic library then Barry Zimmerman's journal paper provides a useful overview (2002).

- Critically consider your curriculum subject knowledge. You might start by auditing your knowledge against a relevant curriculum document. By audit we mean self-assess your subject knowledge against the concepts or topics set out in the curriculum document.

- If a college entrance exam or other test dominates your work as a teacher then you should audit your curriculum knowledge against that, but remember to consider the broader aims of education and the dispositions your learners need for the future as well as the content they need to master to succeed in the test.

- Reflect on your approach to planning and consider how key concepts and meta-learning might become more explicit in your lessons.

References

BBC (2015) *In Our Time*, March 2015. London: British Broadcasting Corporation.

Bell, A. (2013) From No Hope to Nobel. *Times Higher Education Supplement*, 21 March 2013.

Berlin, I. (1969) *Four Essays on Liberty*. Oxford: Oxford University Press.

Blackler, F. (1995) Knowledge, Knowledge Work and Organizations: An Overview and Interpretation. *Organization Studies*, 6, pp 1021–46.

Costa, A. L. and Kallick, B. (2014) *Dispositions: Reframing Teaching and Learning*. London: Sage.

Csikszentmihalyi, M. (2002) *Flow: The Psychology of Happiness. The Classic Work on How to Achieve Happiness*. London: Random House.

de Echevarria, A. and Patience, D. (2008) *Teaching Thinking Pocketbook*. Alresford: Teachers' Pocketbooks.

Duncker, K. (1945) On Problem-Solving. *Psychological Monographs*, 58(5), whole issue.

Gardner, H. (1991) *The Unschooled Mind: How Children Think and How Schools Should Teach*. New York: Basic Books.

Gick, M. L. and Holyoak, K. J. (1980) Analogical Problem-Solving. *Cognitive Psychology*, 12, pp 306–55.

Hattie, J. (2009) *Visible Learning: A Synthesis of Over 800 Meta-Analyses Relating to Achievement*. Abingdon: Routledge.

Higgins, S., Kokotsaki, D. and Coe, R. (2011) *Toolkit of Strategies to Improve Learning: Summary for Schools Spending the Pupil Premium*. Durham: CEM and Durham University.

Hymer, B. and Sutcliffe, R. (2012) *P4C Pocketbook*. Alresford: Teachers' Pocketbooks.

Lewin, K. (1951) *Field Theory in Social Science: Selected Theoretical Papers*, ed. D. Cartwright. New York: Harper and Row.

Lucas, B., Claxton, G. and Spencer, E. (2013) *Expansive Education: Teaching Learners for the Real World*. Maidenhead: Open University Press.

Mansilla, V. B. and Jackson, A. (2011) *Educating for Global Competence: Preparing Our Youth to Engage the World*. Washington, DC: Council of Chief State School Officers EdSteps Initiative and Asia Society Partnership for Global Learning. Available at: http://asiasociety.org/files/book-globalcompetence.pdf (accessed 12 March 2015).

Marzano, R. J., Norford, J. S., Paynter, D. E., Pickering, D. J. and Gaddy, B. B. (2001) *A Handbook For Classroom Instruction That Works*. Alexandria, VA: Association for Supervision and Curriculum Development.

Shulman, L. S. (1986) Those Who Understand: Knowledge Growth in Teaching. *Educational Researcher*, 15(2), pp 4–14. Available at: www.fisica.uniud.it/URDF/masterDidSciUD/materiali/pdf/Shulman_1986.pdf (accessed 20 April 2015).

Stenhouse, L. (1975) *An Introduction to Curriculum Research and Development*. London: Heinemann.

Wang, M., Haertel, G. and Walberg, H. (1993) Toward a Knowledge-Base for School Learning. *Review of Educational Research*, 63(3), pp 249–94.

Zimmerman, B. J. (2002) Becoming a Self-Regulated Learner: An Overview. *Theory into Practice*, 41(2), pp 64–70.

Chapter 5 Feedback versus praise

This chapter is about

- **the unintended consequences of praise on learning and learners;**

- **the use of effective feedback to develop self-regulated learners;**

- **teacher practitioner research as an approach to professional learning and leading change in practice.**

Introduction

Using praise can be helpful in creating a positive environment for learning but it has many drawbacks too. One unintended outcome may be to reinforce a fixed mindset. This chapter proposes that you reflect on power in your relationships with learners and critically appraise the quality of feedback you provide. We focus on how effective feedback might replace praise and prove far more powerful in developing motivated and self-regulated learners.

The dilemma 'feedback versus praise' is relevant both to the achievement of your learners and to your professional development as a teacher. Frequent occurrence of formative assessment with feedback will help to drive your learners' learning. Effective feedback will encourage them to self-assess their own work and become self-regulated learners. Formative assessment will also provide you, the teacher, with useful feedback so that you can consider the question 'What is my impact on learning and learners?' and revise your strategies in response.

This chapter also challenges you to become a self-regulated learner as a teacher by going further than day-to-day inquiry and pursuing longer-term systematic investigation of your impact through collaborative practitioner research. Such a teacher researcher approach provokes interplay between practical wisdom and public knowledge and your findings will provide powerful in-depth feedback on your impact. This kind of feedback is far more useful than the managerialist comments which may be made by a snapshot classroom observer such as a school leader or inspector. Superficial praise on the basis of a lesson observation or a quick analysis of the grades of your learners does not provide you with meaningful feedback about your impact on learning and learners. The dilemma of 'feedback versus praise' also applies to your own professional learning.

CLASSROOM SCENARIO

Helen's parents' evening

Parents' evenings, don't you just love them? I know they're a rare chance to sit down with each parent and talk about their individual child – to offer praise; to nudge things along a bit; or to change things for the better. But, if we're honest, they can be pretty hard going at the end of a long day when you've already done a lot of talking. Still, I gear myself up for them, make sure I know roughly what I'm going to say about each student, I have my mark book in front of me, and I try to limit myself to the five minutes we're supposed to give for each appointment.

I was actually quite looking forward to last week's parents' evening for my class of 15-year-olds. I enjoy teaching this class and I knew I'd have positive messages to say about most of them, so it wouldn't be tough going. In the classroom I have used plenty of praise and created a really positive atmosphere. Most of the class are very bright anyway so their predicted grades are high, based on the school's system of tracking and target-setting, and it is generally easy to find good things to say about their work. There are one or two that really need to get more serious about their studies, so this was a chance to get them back on track. One of the boys I am a little concerned about has got a very supportive mother, so I knew she'd be on my side when I told her he is not making sufficient effort on his homework.

There were just a couple of sets of parents whose reactions weren't exactly what I was expecting. When I saw it was Aleesha's mum pulling up a chair, I was quite pleased. Aleesha is a straight-A student across the board, no different in my subject, and she's worked pretty hard to get there. I was predicting her a B at the start of the year, but she's put in so much effort, and done really well on all her assessments, that she's moved up to an A prediction. I told her mum all of this, and Aleesha was sitting next to her looking pleased with herself. I thought it was a bit tight, therefore, when the mum immediately started asking me how Aleesha could work up to an A* in Year 11. That struck me as a bit pushy, I mean, she's doing well enough to be on the A. I also wasn't really sure what to say. To be honest I'm not sure Aleesha has got that extra bit of sparkle you need for an A*, but how do you say that to her mother? I think I might have mumbled something about her needing to secure her position at the current A and said I'd keep my eye on her, but I'm not sure the mum was all that happy.

And then, straight after that, as luck would have it, Jason's mum and dad arrived. All the data-sets give Jason an A* prediction and when we started the year, I would have thought that a safe bet. I taught him in Year 9 as well and he was a star – full of ideas, a real hard worker. He's taken his foot off the pedal in Year 10 though, coasting a bit, I'd say, thinks he's got it in the bag, so I'd put an A on the report and set some clear targets, and they were what I wanted to talk about during this appointment. His dad actually said to me, 'Well, we're happy with the A – an A is pretty good isn't it? They didn't have these stars when we were at school.' And it was clear they wanted to leave it at that – all very polite and everything, all smiles, but the bit of extra encouragement I was hoping they'd be giving wasn't forthcoming – and really, I'm not sure what I can do about that when there are plenty of other students to worry about.

Back in my classroom the next day, slightly jaded and lacking proper preparation because of the evening shift, I was wondering how my feedback to students on a day-to-day basis is shaped by the school assessment system. The school system is very much based on predicting grades based on standardised tests and then teachers check that learners are 'on track' to achieve that prediction. Is that a good thing, meaning that we have a sensible and coherent school policy, or is it a bad thing because it might have some unintended impact on my students as learners? Typically in a lesson with this class, I try to design a series of learning activities that enable all of the learners to succeed. I provide learning objectives and offer some 'success criteria' and sometimes we work on a piece of exemplar work so they can really start to see what it is I am looking for. This helps to motivate them because they know what to do and can measure their own progress by completing each task in turn. I monitor completion of tasks and use occasional tests to generate grades for my records. The school system requires me regularly to score each student to make sure they are achieving at the expected level and are on track to gain their predicted grade in the exams next year, which is a key gateway for progression to further study.

That's a whole lot of effort that goes into trying to predict what each student will achieve, and even more effort supporting them to achieve that prediction. Yet, in spite of all of that, I am still left feeling uncertain about the extent to which all of this is truly helpful. The reaction of those few parents also wasn't quite what I expected, and if I'm honest, I'm not really sure how I should to react to that. Maybe when I've got further experience, I'll be more savvy about what different parents might expect and how I respond to that, but at the moment I've got more questions than answers.

Questions about Helen's parents' evening

1. What was this parents' evening about? What impact was Helen trying to have on her learners and what was the role of the parents in that?

2. What did the parents seem to make of the meetings and how might they respond? How might Helen change the way she operated in the meetings in order to collaborate with parents in the education of their children?

3. What do we learn about Helen's classroom practice around motivation, challenge and formative assessment? How do the school context and the assessment system seem to be shaping Helen's classroom practice in relation to giving feedback and how might she need to mediate that in order to protect her learners from its unintended influences?

4. What are the implications of this situation for Helen – how might she investigate further the way in which she, her learners and their parents or carers are experiencing and engaging with the different purposes of assessment and feedback?

LEARNING POWER

The learning power of self-regulation

Praise is a powerful influence on learners. Its liberal use by the teacher can create the impression of an encouraging classroom culture. The problem is that praise can influence mindset and its liberal use can undermine the intentions of the teacher. We need to consider how praise might become more usefully framed as feedback. Beyond that, we need to consider what kind of feedback might nurture growth mindsets, thinking dispositions and self-regulated learning.

We want to reinforce the message of this book that derives from the 'learning as construction' vision of learning, rather than the 'learning as acquisition' vision. We have been open about our stance from the outset, but at this point let us 'go meta' and attempt our own compare-and-contrast matrix, incorporating the sometimes competing emphases that we have identified (see Table 5.1).

Table 5.1 Learning as acquisition and (co)construction

Learning as acquisition	Learning as (co)construction
Knowledge is essentially stable and incontestable, and it can be transferred from one person to another	Knowledge is fluid and contestable, and it gets created via the mediation of a learning episode
Knowledge trumps skills	Knowledge and skills are inseparable – there is no dualism
We should seek efficient and well-ordered forms of knowledge transfer, minimising error, doubt and uncertainty	Knowledge construction inevitably requires error, doubt and uncertainty as part of the process, with frequent revisiting of concepts
Ability explains and predicts performance	Beliefs about ability explain and predict performance
Learning is best organized and delivered by the teacher (learner compliance is a virtue)	Learning is best organised and conceived by the learners, but facilitated by the teacher (learner autonomy is a virtue)
Learning is mostly a solitary activity – I learn best by myself	Learning is often a collaborative activity – I can learn well with and from others

Learning as acquisition	Learning as (co)construction
Teaching is a largely technical exercise, involving carefully calibrated inputs and outputs	Teaching requires the exercising of professional judgement in a complex and dynamic context
There is a time and place for abstraction, connection-making and going meta, but curriculum areas tend to be established and bounded within the terms of that discipline	Curriculum boundaries are loose and often arbitrary, and there is value in importing ideas from other areas – this requires metacognitive reflection and transfer
Learning is accelerated and motivated by extrinsic reinforcers – and performance is the goal	Learning is best enhanced by intrinsic reinforcers – and mastery is the goal
Performance indicators help monitor and track learning, keeping it focused	Self-regulation strategies support and lead the learning
Examination results don't lie	Examination results don't lie (but they might be economical with the truth)

We have presented this matrix in the present chapter deliberately, in order to trace a faint, unstated but unmistakable watermark running through the two visions of learning as a whole: the notion of power – who has it, who uses it, and for what ends? If the Hobbesian notion of *scientia potentia est* – knowledge is power – holds force, it should be clear that it is the constructivist vision of learning that seeks purposefully to distribute this power between both teacher and learner, as each brings something essential and meaningful to the creative act of learning.

Praise and other rewards

Nowhere is the potential for a power imbalance more real (and insidious) than in the issue of how learning is incentivised. Within the learning as acquisition vision, it could be argued that learner and teacher enter into a voluntary exchange with mutually beneficial payoffs: I the learner will harness my abilities and efforts in the service of your demands and expectations, and in return you will reward me with praise, merit points and, ultimately, the examination grades to which I aspire and from which we both derive status and gratification. What's not to like?

What's not to like is our conviction that there is no equal exchange going on here. An equal exchange can only take place when there is an assumption – lived out in deeds – that both teacher and learner must be treated with equal dignity and respect as autonomous and rational selves and, in Berlin's terms invoked previously, as being 'conscious of myself as a thinking, willing, active being, bearing responsibility for my choices and able to explain them by references to my own ideas and purposes' (1969, p 131). It is decidedly questionable whether the recipient of a smiley sticker, a merit point, a pencil, a personal judgement ('You're brilliant!') or ten GCSEs could ever be considered to be on equal power terms with the donor. The sentient, free and deeply responsible agent described by Berlin has to act autonomously, *choosing* to work, to strive and to engage of his own volition and not in pursuit of some judge's bounty.

Consider for a moment how often we hear claims along the lines that 'Chloe was *bribed* to work for her exams.' Such claims are technically false, but they betray a deeper truth: we bribe people to do something we and they know they should not do. They are offered to help people over the hump of their consciences or their fear of retribution should justice be served. Chloe clearly therefore wasn't being *bribed:* she was being *rewarded* or *incentivised* (albeit extrinsically and misguidedly – read on) to do something positive. We use the word 'bribe', however, because we know deep down that these extrinsic reinforcers are acts of manipulation, designed to compensate someone for doing something that their better selves might have chosen to do for other reasons: intrinsic motivation, or altruism, or whatever. Incentives are an exercise in the administration of power. Autonomy, trust and respect are their casualties.

You may or may not be convinced by the argument above, which is located in the field of ethics. Rarefied ethical arguments might seem something of a luxury to a beginning teacher facing daily struggles to keep order or to encourage good work habits in their learners. You might prefer something a little less esoteric, a 'Who cares why, does it work?' guide, perhaps?

Let us present then our case from a very pragmatic angle: we have known for over four decades that extrinsic motivators can have a significant and unintended *negative* impact on individuals' intrinsic motivation, especially as measured by individuals' willingness to engage in that activity in their own free time (Deci, 1971; Lepper et al, 1973). Studies in this area report significant achievement gains for those who are *not* rewarded by such extrinsic motivators as money, certificates, stickers and the like, but who are simply encouraged or allowed to find their own satisfactions from the tasks presented. This is not to deny the (very modest) positive effects on intrinsic motivation that incentives can have as measured by learners' *attitudes* towards the activity ($d = 0.14$), and the slightly stronger effect ($d = 0.34$) on learners' abilities to *perform* the 'rewarded' activity (Marzano et al, 2001). Even here though, be cautious: while learners might develop the skill, is this matched by the development of their will? It's the will that gets exposed in those free-time moments: how many learners' literacy skills respond well to the extrinsic motivators of the classroom, but fail to translate into voracious reading habits at home?

In general and rather counter-intuitively, abstract symbolic recognition like well-focused verbal praise (specific, contingent and process- rather than product- or person-oriented) is more effective than tangible rewards. Studies producing the most negative outcomes for incentives tend to use tangible rewards like money, sweets and certificates. But be careful here too: err on the side of frugality when it comes to praise – more does not mean better. Praise (and other rewards) given for accomplishing easy tasks can actually undermine achievement and lower learners' perceptions of their ability (Morine-Dershimer, 1982) because it sets the bar so low.

Watch out too for the desiccating messages that some praise can leave in its wake:

*   'You're a really smart cookie – I'm so proud of you!' *(My value to my mum/dad/ teacher is contingent on my cleverness.)*

- 'You've completed these that fast?! Wow – you must have a mind like a computer!' *(It's all about speed. Not depth, insight, creativity or persistence – speed.)*

- 'Emma you've excelled again – I can always rely on you to produce the goods.' *(What about the first time I fail? It's going to shock her to the core ...)*

- 'I like the way you presented this material – it's really creative.' *(I must do things to impress others.)*

And the other dangers that the wrong sort of praise might risk:

- The invitation to complacency. *(Geniuses always excel, don't they? It's in the nature of fixed genius.)*

- The feeding of resentments. *(Everyone else says I'm brilliant – why don't you, you miserly curmudgeon?)*

- Erroneously locating the purpose of learning with someone else. *(It's my job to make others happy with me and my work.)*

- Seeding a fear of future failure. *(What if I don't deliver this level of performance next time?)*

- Feeding unrealistic self-perceptions of current skill levels. *(Actually, the performance wasn't that great.)*

- Inadvertently diminishing the value of effort and exaggerating the role played by 'natural ability'. *(He was pleased with that?! I wrote that up over breakfast this morning – seems like my brilliance allowed me to BS my way to success again!)*

- Lowering self-perceptions of competence. *(He was pleased with that?! I wrote that up over breakfast this morning – perhaps I'm not capable of anything better? He should know – he's the teacher.)*

- And emphasising the summative at the expense of the formative. *(Seems like where I've been was OK, but where on earth do I go next?)*

Finally, what about those children you teach who don't get any praise at home or in their wider environment? Surely they need you to compensate for this arid emotional climate when they're at school? Actually, it seems that children with low self-esteem are especially susceptible to excessive praise. In a series of both experimental and naturalistic studies, Brummelman et al found that adults are especially inclined to give inflated praise (of the sort, 'That's *incredibly* good work Nathan!') to children with low self-esteem. This inclination may backfire, however. Inflated praise might convey to children that they should continue to meet very high standards, a message that might discourage children with low self-esteem from taking on challenges, causing them to miss out on crucial learning experiences. Inflated praise can backfire with those kids who seem to need it the most (Brummelman et al, 2013).

Though it is deeply embedded in our culture and practice and is therefore certain to remain a staple of the classroom, there are far stronger influences on achievement than external incentives: we have already explored many of these in this book. One of these – quality feedback – can have strong links to the subject of previous chapters, self-regulation.

Feedback

John Hattie's syntheses of meta-studies (2009, 2012) led him to identify the core characteristics of effective feedback:

- It's 'corrective' – ie it provides learners with an explanation of what they're doing right and wrong – but especially right (often neglected in classrooms, as we can assume learners know why they got something right when they don't). Test-like feedback tends to produce weak or even negative effects.

- It's timely – ie generally, delayed feedback leads to delayed progress (one of the reasons for test feedback proving relatively weak).

- It's specific and criterion- (not norm-) referenced – ie it tells learners where they stand relative to the targeted skill or knowledge, not where they stand in relation to others.

- It's invitational – ie learners should increasingly be encouraged to provide their own feedback based on self-assessment. Some of Hattie's very strongest effect sizes relate to interventions which require learners to take control of the setting of personal targets and the prediction of personal grades.

Hattie proceeds to identify four forms of feedback, of which only three lead to significant achievement gains. The fourth, feedback at the level of the self (usually taking the form of praise), does not. For this reason it's questionable whether we should even classify praise as a form of feedback – it provides the learner with none of the three effective forms of feedback:

- *Task* level: How well tasks are understood/performed (eg 'You need to put more about the Treaty of Versailles/toys in Tudor times').

- *Process* level: The process needed to understand/perform tasks (eg 'Try reading this a bit more slowly').

- *Self-regulation* level: Self-monitoring, directing and regulating actions (eg 'You know when you need full stops – check to see if they're needed here').

Nuckles et al (2009) identified a range of prompts as protocols which can serve to enhance the metacognitive demands on learners, helping them to identify and to remediate their own gaps and errors more effectively and more immediately. Slightly adapted, here are a few examples.

Task-level feedback prompts

- Does this answer meet the success criteria?

- Is this right?

- Could you elaborate on this answer?
- What aspect of your response to this assignment are you pleased with/unhappy about?
- What other information do you need to meet the criteria?
- What's the sticking point in this task?

Process-level feedback prompts

- What strategies are you using?
- Are there more efficient strategies you could use?
- What other questions could you ask about this task?
- Do you grasp the concept underpinning this task?
- Have you done anything similar to this before?

Self-regulation-level feedback prompts

- What would be the best way of checking your work?
- How could you reflect on these answers?
- What happened when you ...?
- How can you account for ...?
- What learning goals have you achieved?
- How have your ideas changed?
- What aspect of this work could you now teach to others?

Since the aim of self-regulation feedback prompts such as these is to keep the learning focus with the learner (but simultaneously to help the teacher see this learning through the eyes of the learner, *à la* Hattie), we begin to see hints of what the consummate learner might become: autonomous learners who have developed the cognitive and metacognitive apparatus to become their own teachers. And a learner like this will be rightly bemused when they receive a merit point for handing their homework in, a place on the school's 'gifted and talented' register or even a prize at prize-giving. They won't need your praise or even your criticism. Does a learner like this exist at all? Given the way we construct our school systems, not in huge numbers, but over the course of your career you'll meet a few students like this, those learners who have found a way to put our commonplace but no less egregious practices into perspective. We certainly meet them in adulthood, at the top of their professions, those people who march to their own drum, relatively heedless of others' opinions except in so far as they might learn from them, but working instead to their own high standards of judgement.

Consider the views of successful author Will Self, for instance, as revealed in an interview in the *Guardian Review* as part of a feature on 'Falling Short: Seven Writers Reflect on Failure'. We'll give him the last word here:

> *A creative life cannot be sustained by approval, any more than it can be destroyed by criticism. The criticism has long since ceased to bother me, but the price of this is that the praise is equally meaningless. The positive and the negative are not so much self-cancelling as drowned out by that carping, hectoring internal voice that goads me on and slaps me down all day every day.*
>
> (*Guardian Review*, 22 June 2013)

Things to try

» *To bring the frequency and effects of praise to your consciousness and that of your class, let your class know that you're going to try a praise experiment that lesson/ day/week. During this period, ask them to alert you to the fact that you're issuing praise each time they notice this. You might ask them to suggest an agreed and striking non-verbal symbol for this – for example, raising their hand and repeatedly opening and closing it (in the manner of sun-rays being emitted). Keep a tally. Ask them at the end of the lesson two questions: (1) Did they like being praised? (2) Did that praise help them learn anything, and if so, how and what?*

» *Repeat this experiment with feedback. NB The nature of both praise and feedback will need to be explored with the class before, during and after this experiment, as there will often be confusions and apparent overlaps. This meta-praise and meta- feedback dialogue has value in and of itself, as it supports high-level discussions with your learners about learning, characteristic of most outstanding lessons observed in schools.*

» *Check through some written feedback that you have given to learners on their work or review some school reports on your learners. Treat these text documents as 'data' and analyse them using the critique of practice and the framework for effective feedback offered in this section. In a nutshell, to what extent do the written feedback comments or reports praise effort and strategies used by the learners and to what extent do they offer ways by which they may improve their work in the future? Share your findings with a critical friend and discuss how you might wish to make changes to your practice.*

» *Make a video, if possible, of some of your classroom practice with a focus on questioning and use of feedback. Check the arrangements within your school for making audio or video classroom recordings for the purposes of training. Often parental consent will be in place, but check the detailed conditions for learner consent, use, storage and deletion of the recordings. If it proves too difficult to use video then ask a colleague to observe all or part of your lesson. Using observer feedback or the recording as 'data' analyse your use of praise and other feedback in relation to the framework provided in the 'Learning Power' section above.*

TEACHERS' WORKPLACE LEARNING

The teacher as practitioner researcher

Lawrence Stenhouse (1975) encourages us to continue our lifelong professional learning in the 'art' of teaching. He argues that our ambition as teachers must always be for our learners to go beyond our own level of understanding. We want them to go on to become experts in their future fields of study and work. For Stenhouse, this means that as a teacher you should certainly develop knowledge in curriculum subjects and in pedagogy, but above all that you should pursue a 'mastery of seeking'. By 'mastery of seeking' Stenhouse means expertise in managing your ongoing professional learning through inquiry about your learners, your curriculum subject and your pedagogy. There is widespread support for the development of research-informed practice by teachers but there is considerable debate about what this would look like and how it might be achieved.

For some commentators and policy-makers, research-informed practice by teachers and schools means a focus on public knowledge and the top-down implementation of 'best practice' based on the findings of large-scale quantitative randomised control-trial studies and research meta-reviews. Alternatively, other commentators value action research by teachers because of its situated nature in real school settings, the value it places on practical wisdom and the way that it builds the research capacity of teachers so that they are able to critically evaluate research evidence. Our view is that teachers as professionals need to be able to engage critically with research evidence and identify the implications for their own practice. We believe that teachers are able to contribute to the creation of knowledge through practitioner research. We value a wide range of activity, from the types of teacher inquiry introduced in Chapter 2 to more rigorous, systematic and carefully designed practitioner research studies by teachers that are intended to drive local change in practice and to be disseminated in order to influence other teachers and researchers.

The experience of 'assessment for learning' in schools in England provides a good historical example of the need for teachers and schools to engage critically with a body of research evidence. In this case, a body of research and professional guidance work, helpfully collated through research review and with national support for dissemination, produced only very varied success in influencing practice in classrooms (see eg Marshall and Drummond, 2006). The influence of policy-makers eventually led to considerable distortion of school assessment systems that contradicted the principles of assessment for learning (Mansell et al, 2009). Practitioner research approaches enable teachers to critically evaluate research evidence and take ownership of change in practice.

Well-designed and managed practitioner research projects meet the key characteristics of effective professional learning for teachers: sustained engagement in an issue or intervention over a period of time; a clear focus that is recognised by practitioners to be closely related to raising learners' achievement and well-being; a collaborative learning approach and good levels of trust between practitioners, including an element of classroom coaching; and critical engagement with external knowledge. Such a project provokes interplay between public knowledge and practical wisdom. Practitioner research is a well-established approach to teacher professional development and to leadership of change in schools and, we would argue, forms a key element in the journey towards developing research-informed practice in schools. Within the context of a well-designed research project teachers critically interpret and evaluate 'public knowledge' and consider its relevance to their ways of working, 'practical wisdom', in their particular context. A well-designed teacher research project is able to contribute to practical wisdom and local change in practice and may also contribute to new public knowledge of interest across the field. Overall, a teacher researcher inquiry should ask the question: 'What is my impact on learning and on learners?'

The next section provides seven practical steps towards the design of an effective teacher practitioner research project. Even if you feel that a formal research project is a step too far in your current situation, these seven steps will provide ideas to make your current approach to professional classroom inquiry more systematic and robust.

Seven steps to design your research project

In this section we have outlined seven steps towards creating a well-designed teacher practitioner research project and these are summarised in Figure 5.1. Start at step 1, but there is not a specific order for visiting the other steps. You are likely to visit each step more than once and the idea is to work iteratively, going back and forth. For example, if you develop a research question but then find the data collection would be too time-consuming or difficult, then you will need to revisit some of the other steps to consider and design a more feasible project. You should end up visiting each step more than once until you feel confident that you have a clear research question and a robust, ethical and practicable design. By practicable we mean that it is achievable within the constrained time and other resources that you are able to make available.

In order to make the seven steps more grounded we have referred to an example of a teacher researcher project based in two early years settings in Liverpool and provided some brief quotations from the teacher researchers involved. The project was completed through collaboration between a team of seven teacher researchers and a university-based research mentor and used video to capture interaction between teachers and young children (Boyd, 2014).

1. *The practice-based problem and my purpose*

Use your collective professional judgement, within your practitioner inquiry team, to identify significant problems or areas in need of development within your setting. If you are beginning a project on your own, then look for possible collaborators or at least find a critical friend with whom you can discuss your plans. Your choice of focus may well be influenced by priorities identified by institutional leadership or from external inspectors. However, it is important that

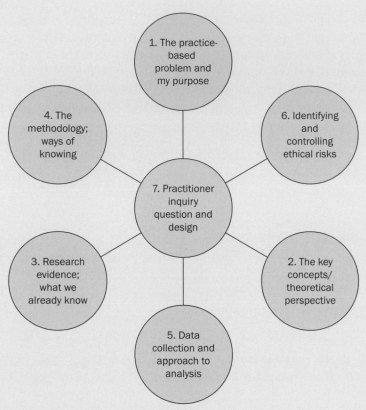

Figure 5.1 *Seven steps for teacher practitioner research project design*

you have some sense of ownership of the inquiry and that you feel it is significant for improving children's learning. In some cases you will be responding to national policy changes or wishing to evaluate the introduction of a new intervention or strategy.

Try to clarify the purpose of the inquiry and consider what its objectives are. For example, what area of practice do you wish to evaluate and improve? Which practitioners and learners do you wish to influence through the inquiry? To what extent will the inquiry rely on and develop trusting collaboration between practitioners? To what extent might you wish to involve parents and carers? To what extent are you aiming to disseminate your findings and how will you do this? As a practitioner researcher you should carefully consider the level of collaboration you might be able to achieve with all stakeholders. Collaboration may be useful in resolving ethical dilemmas and is also likely to strengthen the impact of your study.

> *Having a research team of seven teachers from two schools was helpful because we shared the work of gathering data and learned by analysing each other's ways of working.*
>
> *(Teacher researcher)*

In the teacher researcher project entitled 'Learning Conversations' the focus was on adult–child interactions in early years settings (Boyd, 2014). To some extent this focus was negotiated between leaders of the two schools involved and the research mentor. The teacher researchers were then 'invited' to join the proposed project. It is possible to find examples along a spectrum of control from this top-down approach to the choice of research focus being much more in the hands of the teachers involved.

Your problem issue is likely to be identified in terms of practical wisdom, commonsense ways of working within your work setting. It is therefore important in steps 2 and 3 to critically engage with public knowledge, theory, research evidence, professional guidance and policy, in order to position your emerging research questions in relation to key ideas and what is already known about the issue.

2. The key concepts/theoretical perspective

You should identify and develop an informed view of the key concepts and underlying theory that are involved in your inquiry by critically engaging with relevant public, published knowledge.

In the 'Learning Conversations' project the key concepts involved included 'dialogue' (two-way conversation) and 'sustained shared thinking' (working together to increase understanding). Constructivist learning theory underpins these concepts, broadly meaning that knowledge may be constructed through participation and talking. Together these ideas provided a theoretical framework for the study and influenced the research design.

Key concepts and theory in education are almost always contested, and so it is important that you critically engage with the literature to establish reliable working definitions on which to build your inquiry.

3. Research evidence: what we already know

In developing your inquiry it is important to consider public knowledge, including the research evidence base relevant to your area of inquiry. You should aim to expand your ways of thinking about the issue and to question the assumptions underlying your own practice but also critically evaluate the research and professional guidance literature. This process might be supported by a research mentor and/or by reading research reviews and professional guidance literature. Increasingly, research reviews and papers are available online and open access, but it is still helpful for at least one of your team to have access to an academic library. The relevant research literature may have been interpreted effectively by the author of a high-quality professional guidance text, and such literature is thus also a very useful and accessible way to engage with the research evidence base.

In the 'Learning Conversations' project the considerable body of empirical research on sustained shared thinking and on classroom dialogue underpinned the study and helped us to frame our research questions. There was already considerable evidence to support the learning power of dialogue, but to some extent the evidence base for early years settings is weaker, and this provided an interesting challenge and a gap in the research for us to investigate.

It is tempting and all too easy to skip this crucial step in developing a teacher inquiry. We would argue that without this input of new and external knowledge your inquiry will be seriously weakened and is more likely to lead to weak or even misleading development of teaching.

4. The methodology: ways of knowing

Methodology means a philosophical stance underpinning your inquiry design. How you see the world in relation to the issue you are investigating will affect your choice of data sources and methods. It may help to think of the audience of your project report and what kinds of evidence will persuade them. For example, you may feel that the issue will benefit most from quantitative research and that statistical evidence will provide the most convincing evidence. In this case you may prefer to rely on testing hypotheses using numerical data and statistical analysis, for example, using a pre- and post-test quasi-experimental approach. Alternatively, you may see the issue as an individual or social reality constructed by human perceptions. In this case you may feel that qualitative analysis of narrative data, text data such as transcripts from recorded interviews with teachers or written feedback comments from learners or parents are more appropriate to your inquiry.

> *We found it was essential for us, as teachers, to be involved in analysis of our own data. We were able to provide contextual information about the child and the learning experience.*
>
> *(Teacher researcher)*

Often a mixed methods approach, using numerical and narrative data, will be feasible and may be most effective (Plowright, 2011). In the 'Learning Conversations' project we did not attempt to measure impact on children's speech and language before and subsequent to the change in practice. Further reading on teacher research will help you to select an appropriate approach (Baumfield et al, 2013; EEF, 2015). One consideration in designing a practitioner inquiry is to ensure that you critically consider the wider purpose of education and do not fall into an inquiry design that uses simplistic or easily available measures and merely evaluates classroom techniques (Kemmis, 2006).

5. Data collection and approach to analysis

A great deal of data are available in educational settings but are rarely effectively analysed. These may include statistical records, children's work, teacher planning, lesson observations and policy documents. You might also consider who the stakeholders in your problem area of practice are: children, practitioners, parents and leaders are all possible sources of data. As a practitioner researcher you should carefully consider the level of collaboration you might be able to achieve with all stakeholders. However, you should also take care not to overburden yourself with more data than you need to effectively address the research question.

Methods of data collection include observation, video and audio recordings, surveys, questionnaires, interviews and focus groups. You may consider ways by which children's work creates data, for example, using learning logs or children's drawings. It is helpful to think of gathering four kinds of data from children, including their performance, their feelings, their learning and their thinking (dispositions and metacognition). Consider what insight into the research question the different sources and types of data will provide.

> *The reflection and group analysis twilight sessions were extremely powerful as we had the opportunity to watch video footage and analyse the strategies that we use every day with children.*
>
> (Teacher researcher)

Consider the value of combining different types of numerical and narrative data. For example, using a standardised test in a pre-test and post-test approach may be useful, especially to gain the attention of other practitioners or leaders. It may be equally valuable to gather qualitative data on the perspectives and experiences of children, practitioners and parents or carers. A mixed-methods approach may be worth considering. Your research question(s) may then focus on your impact on learning but also on learners. Always continue to consider the practicability of the data collection and analysis and how it will help you to answer your research question. Be sure to move back and forth between refining your research question and deciding on the data collection methods. In particular, it is important not to become fixed on methods that seem practicable and interesting and neglect the purpose of the study.

6. *Identifying and controlling ethical risks*

It is important to consider ethical issues within your inquiry and formal guidance should be considered by all practitioners (for example, BERA, 2011, available online). Practitioner inquiry requires you to consider the perspectives of participants, those providing data, and other stakeholders involved. The costs, benefits and quality of the research must be considered in deciding if the time and ethical risks for participants are worthwhile. As a researcher you need to plan ways to control any risks to research participants and take steps to reflect on and maintain the ethical approach throughout the project. Universities have formal ethical clearance scrutiny procedures that provide some measure of external reassurance and you may have access to this through a partnership or research mentor. Using video of adult–child interactions in the 'Learning Conversations' project provided powerful data but introduced some ethical challenges that needed careful management.

> *As teacher researchers we selected our own video clips and reflected on these personally before sharing them with the wider team; in this way, each teacher had control and ownership of their own data.*
>
> (Teacher researcher)

It is important to take account of the concept and process of 'informed consent', for example, of parents or carers as well as children, and the right to withdraw data. You need to establish security of data and processes to ensure 'confidentiality' and 'anonymity'. You should also consider how participants might be informed about the emerging findings of the research and possibly comment on them.

7. Practitioner inquiry question and design

Is our research question clear and focused authentically on what we really want to know? Have we planned for systematic gathering and analysis of data? Is our research design likely to provide convincing evidence and lead to change in practice? Is it practicable given the available time and resources? Does it include some measure of children's learning outcomes? Does our design take into account the perspectives of all relevant stakeholders? Have we taken care to control ethical risks to participants, including to the learners and to ourselves as teachers? How will we present and share our findings?

In the 'Learning Conversations' project the research question evolved to become: 'What strategies are teachers using to develop dialogue with young children in early years settings?' The research design involved collection and qualitative analysis of the transcripts of video clips of teacher–child interactions captured using small mobile cameras worn by the teachers during their everyday work.

If your purpose is centred on professional learning and change in classroom practice, as well as on generating new knowledge, then consider to what extent your research design includes the key characteristics of effective professional development for teachers, including: a focus on the impact of practice on learning and learners; sustained involvement; collaboration and trust; an element of classroom coaching; and critical engagement with relevant external public (published) knowledge.

Completing your project

Having designed your teacher inquiry you now need to implement it. It is important to monitor and proactively manage ethical issues throughout the project. The ethical stance of practitioner research creates a powerful framework for professional learning, not least because it can help to develop trust and collaboration as well as resisting managerialism and the high-accountability context in which many teachers are working. Having a clear idea of the purpose of your study and how you plan to disseminate it will help you to make judgements about ethical issues that arise during the study.

Things to try

» *Read research reviews or journal papers relating to areas of interest for you. Browse a research meta-review website resource as an accessible way into particular issues, for example, the Education Endowment Fund Teaching and Learning Toolkit (EEF, 2015). Discuss possible avenues for practitioner research with colleagues in your department or teaching team, or in your wider networks. Consider your current developmental targets and think about whether a small-scale research project would support you in your goals. Remember, your project should be kept small-scale and manageable.*

Reflections on Helen's parents' evening

1.   What was this parents' evening about? What impact was Helen trying to have on her learners and what was the role of the parents in that?

In the busy role of a teacher it is perhaps too easy to think about 'groups' of learners and slightly forget that each learner is an individual with her own story and background. Parents and carers generally are quite rightly focused on children as individuals, and school is a huge part of children's lives – although not the whole story. Helen's parents' evening highlights the potential for close working between teachers and parents/carers but also the challenges of achieving meaningful communication and a collaborative approach.

Expectations and encouragement at home are powerful influences and many individual parents and carers demonstrate fantastic support for their children, including their engagement with school. On the other hand, we know that reducing inequality, poor housing and poverty would make a huge contribution to improving educational outcomes for many children. Education doesn't compensate for society, as Bernstein taught us (2000). Despite all of this, we have to recognise the powerful position we hold as teachers and work towards achieving social justice for our learners. In addition, in most school systems, there is more variation in the influence of teachers within a school than between schools (Hattie, 2012, p 25). The approach of an individual teacher, the beliefs and energy that Helen brings to her teaching, makes a huge difference to learners.

In relation to working with parents there are perhaps two key characteristics of the inspiring teacher that are particularly relevant. First, in creating a positive classroom environment the inspiring teacher develops trust and respect, ensuring that the child wants to learn and that the teacher is committed to helping them and is keen to learn how to do that most effectively. Second, in terms of assessment, the inspiring teacher makes clear their expectations and beliefs that the child can make progress through effort and be successful in their education and wider life. It is important to consider how Helen communicates these aspects of learning to the parents, through her assessment and feedback practice, and to what extent she is able to enlist their support and shape their influence in helpful ways.

Helen does seem to know her learners reasonably well and this fundamental issue requires considerable effort. It is helpful to use seating plans, a focus on the use of names in the first few weeks with a new class, class list photographs, regular informal assessment and good record keeping if you are to get to know your learners as individuals and be able to systematically use and report diagnostic information to support their progress. It is also important to spend time talking to learners informally, to get to know them more fully. It is worth being systematic in making sure that you find time to have conversations with all of your learners, not least to ensure that you are being reasonably equitable. Clearly, such conversations need to be within the boundaries of appropriate professional communication, but conversations with students in which both parties show mutual respect are, of course, perfectly possible to achieve.

In Helen's case it seems that she has done some of this work, she appears to know the students and have some ideas on their strengths and areas for improvement within the subject. A striking point, however, is that she appears to have been very quick to label the students in relation to their level of ability. In this sense she appears to be not only judging their current level of performance but also predicting their future potential. This is a widespread habit, for example, in the UK, but is fundamentally flawed and creates real tensions for Helen in her relationships with the parents and her learners. The approach 'Learning without Limits' is based on a critique of the 'ability labelling' approach, and its application within schools has demonstrated the impact of starting from the assumption that all children can become passionate and engaged learners (Hart et al, 2004; Swann et al, 2012).

Helen comments, 'I'm not sure Aleesha has got that extra bit of sparkle you need for an A*.' This comment suggests that Helen has a fixed mindset perspective. By 'sparkle' we may guess that Helen means some kind of creative flair, but she also seems to be suggesting that you either have this flair from birth or not. This is a commonly heard view in relation to what it takes to achieve the very highest grades, a view that some mysterious inherent quality is needed. It is more appropriate to consider that such flair or sparkle might be developed through effort informed by feedback to develop strategies to improve her work. This positions the 'ability' to show creative flair or sparkle as a disposition or skill that can be developed by a determined learner. The 'Learning without Limits' approach provides a practical rebuff of the underpinning but damaging assumptions held by some educators, parents and educational policy-makers that there are 'clever', 'less clever' and 'not clever' children. It attacks the widespread assumptions too often made that we can judge this innate 'ability' from an early age and make predictions about the level of educational achievement students are capable of reaching.

Overall, Helen might more explicitly view the parents' evening as an opportunity for dialogue with parents and carers in order to collaborate with them in supporting the learners' engagement and progress. Although she appears to have a vague idea of this purpose, she could place more emphasis on listening, on sharing the language of schooling and on modelling and explaining the kind of effective feedback that will best support learning.

2. What did the parents seem to make of the meetings and how might they respond? How might Helen change the way she operated in the meetings in order to collaborate with parents in the education of their children?

Aleesha's mum may come away from the meeting feeling that Helen does not share her high expectations for her daughter. In that case she might feel she has to make even more effort herself to set high expectations and this may not be very helpful to Aleesha. Jason's dad seems likely to come away unaffected by the meeting and still complacent about the potential underachievement of his son (although he does not see it that way).

It would be useful for Helen to consider meetings with parents as an opportunity to gather information as well as providing it. She might have asked how they feel their daughter or son is enjoying school and the subject. An inquiry about homework and a quiet space for study may also have provoked a useful discussion. The key would seem to be to collaborate with parents and value their opinions on the needs of their child. Helen's general approach was quite rightly to provide 'feed forward' on strategies by which her students might improve their work. It is possible to provide some praise of the strengths of a student's work, provided it is specific and avoids comments on the person or a judgement of their 'ability', but rather focuses on the effort or strategy they have used. Helen also identified targets, but perhaps negotiating the targets with the student and their parents would be more appropriate than the teacher deciding on them. Also the targets negotiated may be better focused on strategies and mastery rather than on performance goals. This means that negotiating a target of the student spending the appropriate undisturbed time on homework in a suitable study space might be more useful than getting a particular grade in the next test. This kind of practical target for homework would also draw the parents in and give them a role.

In negotiating with parents it is important that Helen helps them to learn the language of schooling, because this will give them confidence to talk to their child about school and to be able to intervene more assertively, if required, with homework. Parents will have had a wide range of experiences in their own schooling and your classroom practice may be a million miles away from the teaching they experienced. Terms such as learning outcomes, success criteria, learning dispositions, learning to learn, peer assessment and mindset may be a foreign language to many parents, depending on how much regular communication is ongoing within your school.

In Helen's case she is unsure how to handle Aleesha's mum, who seems to be 'a bit pushy' because she is asking what Aleesha can do to achieve an even higher top grade of A*. Given the focus the school is making on grades then it does not seem too unreasonable for Aleesha's mum to ask about this. She seems to be ambitious for her daughter and there is no need for Helen to complain about that; the key seems to be how to make the pressure from her mum into a positive impact on Aleesha. The suggestions for effort and strategies for improvement will vary depending on the subject and on Helen's records concerning Aleesha's current work. In negotiating an action plan it may be possible for Helen to turn parental pressure into practical support. The discussion might include the need for Aleesha to feel generally supported and trusted to work hard. Some consideration of practical ways by which her parents can help Aleesha to work at home will also be useful. A measure of 'effort' might be simply agreed, so that when Aleesha has spent one hour studying in her room then she deserves a reward of a half-hour break. The programme for homework or revision might be discussed and the number of one-hour sessions for each stage working towards the external examinations might be agreed.

Helen has a slightly different issue with Jason's dad, who seems quite happy for Jason to settle for an A when he seems capable of an A*. In this case Helen is convinced that extra effort is the key for Jason to achieve his full potential. In negotiating with Jason and his dad to agree on targets, some simple measures of 'effort' might include 'not getting distracted during lessons' and spending 'at least one hour of quiet study' on his homework. By asking them to agree to such reasonable requests it may be possible for Helen to get Jason back on track.

The issue of complacency needs to be challenged. Jason's dad seems to be satisfied with a good grade rather than expecting Jason to work hard for the top grade. There may be many reasons behind such an attitude and the most important issue for Helen to consider is how his dad's attitude might be influencing Jason's own target setting. Perhaps outlining the choice Jason is making, by settling for a lower grade in this subject, Helen might be able to help him review his decision. She might typically point to the summative role of the examination and grade, although this is likely to seem a fragile line of argument to many 15-year-old boys. It is important for Helen to consider and show awareness of the importance of the wider interests and activities of the learner beyond school, because it is possible to create too much pressure around grades. By suggesting strategies that would enable Jason to continue to pursue his wider interests but still aim higher in his schooling, Helen might be able to bring his dad on board.

Feedback versus praise. In Helen's case, she was dealing with very successful learners and in some ways that can be tricky. It is too easy to simply lay on heavy general praise for such successful children and help to nurture fragile and fixed mindsets that would leave them vulnerable in the future when faced with learning challenges. On the other hand, parents may have come to expect parents' evenings to be a warm, bubbly bath of delighted praise for their hard-working and compliant children. With all parents it is important to make very clear that you know their child well and to start and perhaps finish the conversation with specific positive comment on some aspect of the child's effort or strategies. Then you must move on to feedback, and that feedback should provide specific strategies that the child might use to improve their work. With generally hard-working or high-achieving children, as in Helen's case, you should demonstrate trust that they will wish to aim really high and an expectation that they are capable of continuing to improve. It is sometimes difficult to identify within an excellent piece of work ways that it could be improved. However, if that is occurring frequently in your classroom then clearly you need to raise the bar and set more open-ended and challenging tasks that allow all of your children to be stretched. In preparing to meet parents it will be useful to reflect back on children's responses and achievements on these kinds of tasks and check your mark book and other records. Perhaps Helen might look closely at the examination assessment criteria and guidance to understand more about the difference between an A and an A*.

The emphasis of the school assessment system on target grades and the wider social context that highlights external examination grades as the key goal of schooling influences parents as well as teachers. Parents are likely to come to the meeting with a teacher expecting grade predictions. While satisfying this expectation, Helen should also take the opportunity to focus on strategies for improvement and encouraging the learner, with the support of their parents, to set high goals.

3. **What do we learn about Helen's classroom practice around motivation, challenge and formative assessment? How do the school context and the assessment system seem to be shaping Helen's classroom practice in relation to giving feedback and how might she need to mediate that in order to protect her learners from its unintended influences?**

It might be useful if Helen could consider her assessment as a source of feedback on the effectiveness of her teaching. By that we mean that her assessment of learners' work might be treated as 'data' to help her consider the question 'What is my impact on learning and learners?' In analysing those data we would accept that on a day-to-day basis Helen would mainly be operating within the horizontal knowledge domain of practical wisdom. This would involve Helen considering very pragmatic changes to her practice: 'Many of the class did not seem to have grasped that key idea so I need to revisit it, perhaps using a different strategy.' By going further and relating her emerging findings to public, published knowledge, Helen will create an opportunity for professional learning through interplay and have a chance to make a more research-informed change in practice.

Many school systems have developed well-intended assessment and target-setting processes that shape the approach adopted by teachers and parents and profoundly influence children's beliefs about their 'ability'. These systems are often deeply flawed and may distort the beliefs of children, teachers and parents in unhelpful ways. It is not surprising that Helen, embedded in the system, seems happy to label children in terms of ability. Her school appears to support this kind of assessment and prediction approach, which has been developed for monitoring the progress of groups of pupils for quality assurance purposes but requires considerable mediation to make it appropriate for use with individual learners and their parents.

Clearly, parents will want to know about the current performance of their child, and in contexts where students are working towards an important summative external test or exam parents often want to know the current grade they are working at. The key is to frame that information within a feedback focus on effort and strategies for improvement. Praise from the teacher will be useful when applied to specific examples of effort and the use of effective strategies by the student. In effect this is saying 'keep on giving more of the same, please'. Targets should then be negotiated through discussion with the student and their parents and focus on specific increased effort and new strategies for improvement. Introducing a specific 'predicted' or 'target' grade that is based on aggregated figures for the past performance of students with a similar current profile seems unlikely to be statistically justifiable and would at the very least need a careful qualifying statement that may just go straight over the student's head. Such figures rely on the meaningfulness of the test results gathered so far and aggregate the effort made by students at each stage of the game. It might be more honest and effective to report that based on the average performance of previous students with a similar test result profile your daughter/son is currently making steady progress, underperforming or exceeding typical progress. If Helen's school requires her to provide 'predicted' grades to parents and learners, then at least she can try to mediate their impact by explaining the limitations of the statistics underpinning them.

In some countries, and in some UK schools that have adopted alternative approaches, there is much more emphasis placed on cultural influence and agency than on the idea of innate 'ability'. This allows a school approach based on the assumption that there is 'always the potential for change' on the basis of what teachers and learners do (Swann et al, 2012, p 5). Three principles of 'co-agency',' trust' and 'everybody' were developed in the 'Learning without Limits' approach. 'Co-agency' is about children and teachers working together and focuses on increasing the autonomy of learners and their commitment to the learning opportunities provided. 'Trust' is a principle that all children want to learn and they can become enthusiastic learners if provided with relevant and purposeful learning activities. Finally, the principle 'Everybody' is about teachers and schools committing to the interests of all learners, not particular individuals or groups of learners. This includes a commitment to building a learning community in which all members help each other.

Helen is an individual teacher working within a particular school and educational system. It may seem unfair and even petty to criticise her use of ability labelling in the context of this parents' evening. But this is a fundamental issue: if she feels comfortable using such fixed mindset ideas in the context of a parents' evening, it suggests that these reveal her underpinning beliefs and will strongly influence her practice and her impact on learning and learners. It means she is making assumptions about the limits on individual learners and is likely to be expressing lower expectations for some individuals through her informal, day-to-day classroom communication. No doubt, if challenged on this issue, Helen is likely to fall back on appeals to be 'realistic' and 'not raising hopes too high'. However, there is a huge list of people who have 'failed' at school only to be hugely or quietly successful in their later lives. In addition, we know that persistent effort is the key to progress in learning, and Helen's labels are based on current and past behaviour of her students whereas they may be able to change in the future.

Helen is not able to change the wider education system and will only be able to influence her school's systems through sustained collaboration with colleagues. However, she is able to mediate some of the effects of national and institutional assessment systems by adopting a formative assessment approach with effective feedback that focuses on effort and strategies and supports the development of self-regulated learners.

4.   **What are the implications of this situation for Helen – how might she investigate further the way in which she, her learners and their parents or carers are experiencing and engaging with the different purposes of assessment and feedback?**

At least two broad, interrelated questions seem to arise from the scenario of Helen's parents' evening:

• To what extent does the school's assessment system promote formative assessment and how do individual teachers mediate the school system for their learners?

• How does the school work collaboratively with parents to develop shared understanding and language around formative assessment and effective feedback?

As a beginning teacher Helen would realistically need to focus on her own priorities and goals for improving her practice and perhaps might rephrase these school-level research questions into more manageable inquiries.

In relation to the question above on school assessment systems, Helen might consider 'To what extent does my written feedback on learners' work include comment on the task, the process and on supporting self-regulation?' In this case her written feedback as a source of data is already easily available, but she might need to collect other data, for example, if she wishes to consider how her written feedback is experienced by the learners and how it relates to numerical measures of achievement such as the grades awarded or test results.

In relation to the broad question about how the school works with parents, the scope of the relevant existing research evidence is not substantial. Having reflected on the parents' evening Helen might consider using an action research approach by making an intervention, a change in her practice, and then evaluating its impact. Helen might ask 'How effectively am I communicating and collaborating with parents to support students in their learning and progress?' She might start to develop communication with parents, perhaps via her learners.

Critical engagement with public knowledge (learning theory, research evidence, professional guidance and policy) is a crucial element of these proposed practitioner research projects. Increasingly, you will be able to find relevant public knowledge online. There are some useful online summaries of research aimed at teachers and research meta-review websites such as the *Teaching and Learning Toolkit* (EEF, 2015) provide powerful, accessible and well-designed tools. It is important to read the 'how to use this resource' section of such a resource and to critically consider the limitations of research meta-review evidence.

The key for Helen is to capture the immediate reflective learning from her experience of the parents' evening and to turn that into a more sustained inquiry-based project that is closely integrated with her developing practice and everyday work.

Chapter 5 summary

This chapter has focused on the dilemma 'feedback versus praise', which may seem controversial given the considerable emphasis there has been on giving praise to develop a positive learning environment and to manage behaviour.

Learning power

- Extrinsic rewards, stickers and prizes may have a negative effect on learners, especially when the aim is for them to continue that activity in their own time. It is better to encourage learners to find their own satisfactions.

- Well-focused verbal praise is reasonably effective, but it must be specific and focused on strategies and effort, rather than on the person or the product.

- High-quality feedback is a powerful driver for learning. Feedback may usefully include suggestions on how to improve the work, comments on how to adjust the process and prompts for self-regulation.

Teachers' workplace learning

- Developing collaborative practitioner research by teachers is an effective approach to continuing professional learning and leading change in practice if it is sustained, collaborative, involves experimentation in the classroom and includes critical engagement with the vertical domain of public, published knowledge.

- In developing research-informed practice there is value in considering research findings based on randomised control trials and on meta-reviews of research evidence, but the limitations of that evidence base also need to be acknowledged.

- In developing research-informed practice, knowledge creation is possible through robust practitioner research by teachers in classrooms and schools.

Taking it further

* In relation to developing feedback to nurture growth mindsets, it is worth revisiting Chapter 2 and the suggestions for further study there.

* In relation to the use of praise and other reward systems in school, we recommend *Praise, Motivation and the Child* by Gill Robins (2012).

* In relation to feedback within the wider issue of formative assessment, a good starting point might be the *Assessment and Learning* Teachers' Pocketbook (Smith, 2014). We strongly recommend Shirley Clarke's excellent and very practical guide to formative assessment (Clarke, 2014). Another useful book on formative assessment is by Bill Boyle and Marie Charles (2014).

* For further development of teacher practitioner research, we recommend the practical guides to teacher research by Lankshear and Knobel (2004), which is thoughtful and comprehensive, by Koshy (2005), which is helpfully practical and accessible, or by Baumfield et al (2013), which is more recent.

References

Baumfield, V., Hall, E. and Wall, K. (2013) *Action Research in Education* (2nd edn). London: Sage.

BERA (British Educational Research Association) (2011) *Ethical Guidelines for Educational Research.* London: BERA

BERA (British Educational Research Association) (2014) Research and the Teaching Profession: Building the Capacity for a Self-Improving Education System. Available at: www.bera.ac.uk/ project/research-and-teacher-education (accessed 20 February 2015).

Berlin, I. (1969) *Four Essays on Liberty*. Oxford: Oxford University Press.

Bernstein, B. (2000). *Pedagogy, Symbolic Control and Identity: Theory, Research, Critique* (rev. edn). London: Rowman & Littlefield.

Boyd, P. (2014) 'Learning Conversations: Teacher Researchers Evaluating Dialogic Strategies in Early Years Settings. *International Journal of Early Years Education*, 22(4), pp 441–56.

Boyle, B. and Charles, M. (2014) *Formative Assessment for Teaching and Learning*. London: Sage.

Brummelman, E., Thomaes, S., Overbeek, G., Orobio de Castro, B., van den Hout, M. A. and Bushman, B. J. (2013) On Feeding Those Hungry for Praise: Person Praise Backfires in Children with Low Self-Esteem. *Journal of Experimental Psychology*: Advance online publication. doi: 10.1037/ a0031917.

Clarke, S. (2014) *Outstanding Formative Assessment: Culture and Practice.* London: Hodder.

Deci, E. L. (1971) Effects of Externally Mediated Rewards on Intrinsic Motivation. *Journal of Personality and Social Psychology*, 18, pp 105–15.

EEF (Education Endowment Foundation) (2015) *Teaching and Learning Toolkit.* Sutton Trust. Available at: http://educationendowmentfoundation.org.uk/toolkit/toolkit-a-z/ (accessed 11 March 2015).

Hart, S., Dixon, A., Drummond, M. J. and McIntyre, D. (2004) *Learning without Limits*. Maidenhead: Open University Press.

Hattie, J. (2009) *Visible Learning: A Synthesis of Over 800 Meta-Analyses Relating to Achievement*. Abingdon: Routledge.

Hattie, J. (2012) *Visible Learning for Teachers: Maximising Impact on Learning*. Abingdon: Routledge.

Kemmis, S. (2006) Participatory Action Research and the Public Sphere. *Educational Action Research*, 14(4), pp 459–76.

Koshy, V. (2005) *Action Research for Improving Practice: A Practical Guide*. London: Sage.

Lankshear, C. and Knobel, M. (2004) *A Handbook for Teacher Research: From Design to Implementation*. Maidenhead: Open University Press.

Lepper, M. R., Greene, D. and Nisbett, R. E. (1973) Undermining Children's Intrinsic Interest with Extrinsic Reward: A Test of the 'Overjustification Hypothesis'. *Journal of Personality and Social Psychology*, 28, pp 129–37.

Mansell, W., James, M. and the Assessment Reform Group (2009) *Assessment in Schools: Fit for Purpose? A Commentary by the Teaching and Learning Research Programme*. London: Economic and Social Research Council, Teaching and Learning Research Programme. Available at: www.tlrp.org/pub/documents/assessment.pdf (accessed 5 February 2015).

Marshall, B. and Drummond, M. J. (2006) How Teachers Engage with Assessment for Learning: Lessons from the Classroom. *Research Papers in Education*, 21(2), pp 133–49.

Marzano, R. J., Norford, J. S., Paynter, D. E., Pickering, D. J. and Gaddy, B. B. (2001) *A Handbook for Classroom Instruction That Works*. Alexandria, VA: Association for Supervision and Curriculum Development.

Morine-Dershimer, G. (1982) Pupil Perceptions of Teacher Praise. *Elementary School Journal*, 82, pp 421–34.

Nuckles, M., Hubner, S. and Renkl, A. (2009) Enhancing Self-Regulated Learning by Writing Learning Protocols. *Learning and Instruction*, 19, pp 259–71.

Plowright, D. (2011) *Using Mixed Methods: Frameworks for an Integrated Methodology*. London: Sage.

Robins, G. (2012) *Praise, Motivation and the Child*. Abingdon: David Fulton/Routledge.

Smith, I. (2014) *Assessment and Learning Pocketbook* (2nd edn) Alresford: Teachers' Pocketbooks.

Stenhouse, L. (1975) *An Introduction to Curriculum Research and Development*. London: Heinemann.

Swann, M., Peacock, A., Hart, S. and Drummond, J. (2012) *Creating Learning without Limits*. Maidenhead: Open University.

Chapter 6 Collaboration versus competition

Though people can think for themselves, they cannot think by themselves.
(Stenhouse, 1967, p 119)

This chapter is about

* **the learning power of collaboration;**

* **ways in which collaborative learning may take place within schools (between learners and between teachers).**

Introduction

In this chapter we explore the learning benefits of collaboration for both teachers and their learners. These benefits relate to learning as well as to engagement and social skills. The chapter will consider the evidence that co-operative working, peer support and discussion all promote learning in classrooms.

It is possible to experience teaching as a fairly isolated profession. This may seem strange given that for much of the day you have around 30 learners in your classroom and perhaps even a teaching assistant. But in terms of having time to talk to colleagues, a typical busy school day might speed by with only a few snatched interactions with other adults. However, it is possible to avoid a sense of isolation by adopting a determinedly proactive and collaborative approach. Many schools have a very strong sense of community spirit, but even if the atmosphere of your current workplace does not lend itself to meaningful interaction between adults, we urge you to identify colleagues whom you can get to know better, and start to engage with them in the hope of nurturing at least one critical friend on the staff.

CLASSROOM SCENARIO

Sammie's science lesson

Group work is good. This is a truth universally acknowledged. At least it is on my teaching training course, and by my headteacher and by practically everyone I know who teaches in a modern classroom. In many primary schools these days, children are used to sitting together in groups, and working together on various activities. We like group work, we think people observing our lessons like group work. We assume most of our students like group work. However, I'm starting to ask myself what it is really all about – I'm not sure I really know what I want to happen when I get students to talk to each other. OK, so they are sitting together in groups, but does that tick the box that says, 'I'm doing group work', and even if it does, is that all it is doing?

When I started teaching whole classes independently, I thought something along the lines of, 'What, I'm just learning how to control a class when they are all sitting calmly and I can more or less see what's going on! You mean you want me to make them stand up, move around so they are not sitting next to the people they normally sit next to? And on top of that you want me to tell them I want them to TALK to each other!' Still, I knew it was what was expected, and I had to start thinking about group dynamics and teaching strategies rather than just letting it happen. My first lessons went OK, I suppose: no major incidents occurred. When I was expecting students to collaborate in groups it got a bit noisier than I thought it should be, but the tasks pretty much got done. I'm not so unsettled by the thought of group discussions now: I realise that is part of the dynamics of the classroom, but I'm still not sure what I really want to happen when I plan sessions where students are working together in groups.

So last week, my teacher mentor in school suggested that I should step it up a bit, and be a bit more ambitious in the group work I was planning. He suggested that a session I was planning this week would be a good opportunity for me to rearrange the class into different groups and think about how I wanted them to work collaboratively. My heart sank a bit, to be honest. This was for a science lesson on 'changing materials' and there was already a lot for me to think about before I even turned my attention to the group aspect. The idea was to look at a variety of common materials – paper, stone, tin foil, cotton, a waterproof coat, plastic – and think about how they would behave under particular circumstances. We would experiment with different situations – water, heat, cold – the children would think about how they would expect the materials to behave, undertake the experiment, then reflect on the results and write them up. As it involved a lot of resources, and had some health and safety issues on top of everything else, my plan was to conduct the experiments myself at the front, with some carefully chosen helpers for some parts. Then the children would move into groups and write up the results. My mentor seemed happy with this idea – we could control the experiments pretty much, and the group work element would still be intact in the second part of the lesson.

Thankfully, it all went according to plan. The class loved watching the experiments. I was delighted with the number of hands being put up to guess what would happen when I put each material in the tray of water. The transition into the groups went pretty smoothly. I had already grouped the tables and chairs; I had formulated the groups in advance based on assessment data (these mainly come from numeracy and literacy tracking). I had differentiated to provide more structured worksheets for the lower-ability groups; I had designated a group leader for each table.

Their task was to use the piece of sugar paper on each table to record and present the findings of the experiments as a poster. I had given them images or samples of each material we had used, and I'd organised a box of coloured pens, glue sticks and scissors on each table in advance. I modelled an example of what the outcome should look like from the front, and I had put a vocabulary list on each table with key words from the experiments. I had to tell them a couple of times to keep the noise down, but mostly it was OK and, as I moved around helping each group, I made sure they were staying on task. I was also lucky to have the teaching assistant working with the lowest-ability group, and she gave them lots of support so they could complete a poster alongside everyone else. It was all a bit of a rush at the end, and I had to let the children go out to break and then clear up the resources from their tables. I didn't beat myself up too much about that, though. I wanted to let them finish their posters, so even though there was a bit of tidying up for me to do, they'd been able to spend the time getting things finished. Three girls in one group even stayed in for the first ten minutes of break to get their poster done.

So, I have every reason to be pretty pleased with myself, right? There was nothing wrong with any of this: plain sailing? Well, I thought so during the lesson, and even when I first looked at the six finished posters I collected in at the end. They all looked attractive: good visual impact – I knew they would look great on the wall. I was glad each group seemed to have let the neat writers do the headings, and some of the children had clearly loved designing the heading 'Materials' in pretty colours; they were so enthusiastic about it. Each group had used the vocabulary sheet, and all of them had correctly remembered the results of the experiments. But after the first ten minutes of looking at the children's work, something didn't sit right. True, I had six posters that displayed accurate knowledge and would look good on the wall. But did I really have any more than that? Was that enough? Had I made the most of the group work and what had been the point of it? I could pat myself on the back that it had all gone smoothly, but, looking at the work produced by the children, I was not so sure the lesson was as good as I had thought at the time.

Questions about Sammie's lesson

1. What was the purpose of the group work? Did each person in the group feel they had a shared purpose, and that they would be individually accountable for their contribution? Is the group task any more than a presentation? Would a learner who had designed an attractive title for the group poster think that he had succeeded in this group task? Did group work strengthen the progress of learners during the lesson?

2. We know that some of the children really enjoyed the activities in the lesson. How should the teacher balance this enjoyment in evaluating the effectiveness of the lesson?

3. Do these children know how to work together in groups? Have the expectations of group interaction been made clear? Do the children think it matters how they work together in the group? Were they directed to review their group work in any way?

4. Does the teacher seem to make the best use of the support provided by the teaching assistant? If the teaching assistant had been off sick that day, then how might that have affected the impact of grouping the learners? Is ability grouping a good idea?

5. To what extent does Sammie seem to be collaborating with the teacher mentor? How might this relationship be developed by Sammie to become more productive in terms of professional learning?

LEARNING POWER

The learning power of working together

> *None of us is as smart as all of us.*
>
> (K. H. Blanchard)

The scholar Martin Buber taught us that 'All real living is meeting' (Buber, 1958, p 25). Humans are social animals, so it should be little surprise that the social dimension is a key player in teaching and learning: we learn with and through others, or, as Lawrence Stenhouse put it, though we can and should think *for* ourselves, we cannot think as well *by* ourselves (Stenhouse, 1967). This insight lies at the heart of constructivism, and it lies specifically at the heart of the teacher–learner relationship. Though our emphasis so far has been on classroom applications of educationally invaluable but rather abstract processes like autonomy, feedback and metacognition, there are reciprocal benefits flowing between these vital processes and outstanding human relationships. One early career secondary English teacher made these benefits explicit in a headily exuberant email, describing the unexpected gifts arising from good pedagogy:

> *I have been including your suggestions in my teaching. They had immediate and significant effects on learning and (something I did not predict) greatly improved my relationships with students. I know them so much better because they communicate their ideas to me rather than the other way round – and they inform me about what they learn and how they learn it. This is true of all ages and abilities. It's truly inspiring to have such stimulating relationships with my students. We are all so motivated in our joint learning, it's fantastic!*
>
> *(E. T., personal communication to one of the authors)*

This email, written back in 2008, beautifully anticipates Hattie's description of 'visible learning', that golden state of unity between teacher and learner such that both shift seamlessly from one role to another, the teacher seeing with lucid clarity what the learner sees and the learner becoming her own teacher.

Great teacher–learner relationships are, of course, only one form of classroom collaboration. Teachers who routinely engineer their classroom practices to include significant elements of focused social interaction reap a rich bounty, as revealed by the meta-study synthesisers:

- Robert Marzano et al (2001) report effect sizes ranging from 0.30 to 0.78 (percentile gains from 12 to 28) for co-operative learning.

- Steve Higgins et al (2011) report potential gains for peer-assisted learning of six months-plus (> $d = 0.5$ – ie one GCSE grade) and *high impact at low cost*.

- John Hattie (2009, 2012) cites an exceptional effect size of 0.82 for classroom discussion – one of his most powerful influences on achievement (and one that can most easily be developed in all classrooms).

Though co-operative learning, peer-assisted learning and discussion are by no means identical in their classroom manifestations, the presence of intentional verbal exchanges is a common currency, and they do all bear witness to the power of classrooms as 'learning communities' (Watkins, 2005), with learners supporting the learning of their peers rather than seeing their peers as rivals to their own learning and achievement. This distinction mirrors the 'acquisition' versus 'construction' metaphors of learning that we explored in Chapter 1, and which run like a thread throughout this book. When learning involves acquiring new and uncontested knowledge and skills, then those learners with the greatest abilities and most absorbent and retentive memories might be expected to learn at the greatest rate. And this need not involve any other learner. On the contrary, other and perhaps 'less able' learners might act as an unwelcome impediment or brake to learning, and 'more able' learners serve merely to remind the individual of his more modest abilities. In this condition, competition between learners is inevitable, and may even be desirable as a motivational spur.

But when learning is an act of deliberate co-construction, and 'ability' loses its status to metacognitive processes and such learning dispositions as persistence, graft, and giving and receiving support to and from others, then co-operation rather than competition with peers becomes the sensible option to pursue. Others' learning and achievement successes don't diminish one's own: they are more likely to provide models to enhance it. As expressed pithily by Roseth et al (2006), if you want to increase student academic achievement, give each student a friend. And as we saw in Chapter 4, Hattie provides substantial evidence for the value of learning with and through others, noting that when challenge levels are high, learners' metacognitive skills rather than their 'ability' become the best determinant of the quality of their learning outcomes (Hattie, 2009, p 30). And how best are learners' metacognitive skills developed? By engaging in sustained and frequent internal and external dialogic exchanges around learning.

The Japanese have an expression that translates roughly as 'No one's as smart as we all are smart', and in this can be found the power of collaboration: we learn from and with each other – by hearing, advancing and interrogating ideas in dialogue with others, shaping and improving them in the process, not just by casting further into the net of our own minds. Vygotsky, one of the most influential social constructivists of all time, famously observed that:

> *Every function in the child's cultural development appears twice: first, on the social level, and later, on the individual level; first, between people (interpsychological) and then inside the child (intrapsychological). This applies equally to voluntary attention, to logical memory, and to the formation of concepts. All the higher functions originate as actual relationships between individuals.*

(Vygotsky, 1978, p 57)

There is other strong evidence for the advantages of co-operation over competition in the classroom:

• Johnson et al's seminal research synthesis (1981) reported impressive gains for co-operative learning in general ($d = 0.73$).

• Other research syntheses have also been supportive, including Walberg (1999), $d = 0.78$, and Lipsey and Wilson (1993), $d = 0.63$ – percentile gains from 23 to 28!

• Johnson et al (1981) found the largest effects of co-operative learning on achievement to be when co-operative learning was compared with approaches involving students competing with each other ($d = 0.78$ – percentile gains of 28) or with students engaged in individual tasks (again, $d = 0.78$).

• Hattie's synthesis of meta-studies (2009, p 212) provides further evidence that co-operative learning trumps simply having heterogeneous (mixed) classes ($d = 0.41$), and is superior to individualistic learning ($d = 0.59$) and to competitive learning ($d = 0.54$), but that competitive learning is somewhat superior to individualistic learning ($d = 0.24$).

In summary: peers are powerful agents of and resources for learning!

Group work

So if co-operative learning is as powerful as all these studies suggest, what exactly does it look like in the classroom? More specifically, what would it look like in your classroom? One of the weaknesses of meta-reviews of research is that they signal the impact on learning of a broad category of intervention, but as a teaching team you need to reconstruct the intervention in your particular school and with your particular learners. To understand better the core features of co-operative learning it's worth considering the compare-and-contrast formulation offered by Johnson and Johnson (1999) (see Table 6.1).

It's no accident that most of the characteristics of co-operative learning identified in the table resonate with the key teaching strategies proposed in this book, not least the emphases on dialogic feedback (central to the facilitative teacher's role), reciprocity, the valuing of the process as well as the product, and metacognition (review/processing). It is these features, especially when working in concert, that bring the effects on achievement reported in the meta-study syntheses.

Table 6.1 *The characteristics of traditional and co-operative group work*

Traditional group work	Co-operative group work
Minimal interdependence	Active interdependence
Limited individual accountability	Significant individual accountability
Largely homogeneous (similar) membership	Largely heterogeneous (mixed) membership
One leader (appointed or emerged)	Distributed leadership
Emphasis on the task (product)	Emphasis on the task and relationships (product and process)
Social skills assumed or ignored	Social skills directly taught
Directive teacher role	Facilitative teacher role
Limited group review/processing	Significant group review/processing

To enable co-operative learning through interaction, both teachers and learners need to develop their skills to achieve meaning-making through dialogue. Neil Mercer argues that teachers need to focus on 'language as a means for collective thinking' and proposes the term 'interthinking' as an alternative or extension to 'interaction' (Mercer, 2000). There has been a considerable body of research and development work focused on 'sustained shared thinking', meaning that the participants in a conversation work together in an intellectual way to solve a problem (Sylva et al, 2004). A range of strategies that help teachers to develop dialogue include: building on the child's interests; recasting; extending; questioning; allowing thinking time; making connections; introducing new vocabulary; and aiming to achieve a balanced dialogue despite the teacher's position of power (Alexander, 2004; DCSF, 2008).

Learning in groups

There is a caution to be sounded though, when it comes to the issue of organising for collaborative and co-operative learning: the concept of 'ability' brings nothing of value to the party, and it may work against it. We explored the limitations and dangers of fixating on ability in Chapter 2, but it's worth revisiting it here specifically in the context of how we organise and structure our classes and groupings within classes. One of the reasons grouping for co-operative learning trumps other forms of grouping (and no grouping at all) is the element of heterogeneity (how mixed the groups are): in heterogeneous groups, with a complete mix of learners, offering a wide diversity of skills, interests and experiences, the potential for peer learning is far richer than it is in groups which have already been filleted and graded, on the basis of assessments of dubious predictive reliability, to ensure a degree of homogeneity. Nature teaches us to value diversity and resilience, not efficiency, but in social formations we rarely invite nature to be our teacher – we seek efficiencies. And at our cost.

As a consequence of our system's privileging of efficiency over diversity, you may have little power to ensure heterogeneity in your current school's classes. Ability grouping is very popular with politicians (and sometimes also with school inspectors) because of its historical heft and its populist appeal, especially to the parents of 'top set' children. But it's worth admitting that it's also overwhelmingly popular with schools and with teachers: it is often easier to prepare for and to teach a relatively homogeneous group of learners. But the empirical evidence suggests it does very little for most learners and nothing at all for some (the lower sets). Therefore, you would do well to retain a critical eye on the structures within your own school or department and do all you can to mitigate the worst effects of policy decisions that fall beyond your reach: in all classes, setted and unsetted, exploit every opportunity for peer learning and collaboration. Seek to structure five core elements into small-group work (Bennett et al, 2005):

1. **positive interdependence:** all members feel connected in the pursuit of a common goal, and all must succeed for the group to succeed;

2. **individual accountability:** each member is held responsible for the accomplishment of the learning;

3. **face-to-face interaction:** to maximise linguistic exchanges;

4. **social skills:** turn-taking, encouraging, listening, clarifying, probing, help-giving, etc;

5. **group processing:** joint assessment of their efforts and targeting of improvements.

In general, be sparing in your use of ability groups (but these are better than no grouping), keep groups small (three to five), and find a balance between consistent use and over-use.

And if your school makes the brave but evidence-based decision to undo ability grouping – what in the USA is called 'detracking' – be aware that this alone seems not to lead to any significant improvements in learning and achievement (Rui, 2009), except for lower sets, where the worst effects of setting are to be found. As we've seen above, the power of social and linguistic interaction among peers is strong, and even ability groups can confer some of these benefits when compared with learners working alone. So undoing ability grouping is advised, but it must be combined with a relentless focus on the quality of the teaching and exploitation of the peer learning potential in heterogeneous (mixed) classrooms. And the impact on learning and learners should be monitored.

Things to try

»   *Here are a few classroom approaches that you might wish to explore in your quest to harvest the fruits of lessons that consistently include significant elements of co-operative learning:*

- *Logo-Visual Teaching: A tool for making meaning through the physical manipulation of ideas in small groups – embracing both talk and the movement of thoughts and ideas captured on Post-it notes or similar.*

- *Philosophy for Children (P4C): An approach to learning that involves participants generating their own questions from a stimulus, choosing one question to focus on and being led through a philosophical inquiry into that question by a skilled facilitator.*

- *The Jigsaw Method: A tool for learning that requires participants to become experts in a part of the whole, then recombining into new groups to share their own expertise, and in turn to be taught the expertise of other members of their group so that they ultimately have a good grasp of the whole area.*

- *Team Mindmaps: A process whereby small groups of learners create a visual representation of the unit being studied, moving out from the core concepts to the peripheries of the concrete examples.*

- *PMI: A thinking tool in which participants identify the Positives (Plus), Negatives (Minus) and the contestable (Interesting) elements of any proposal, statement or invention.*

Take care to refer back to the principles of co-operative learning discussed in this section as you develop new classroom strategies and activities.

TEACHERS' WORKPLACE LEARNING

Teacher learning communities

Teaching is a challenging profession involving cognitive and emotional labour in managing working relationships with learners and with other stakeholders. Strong working relationships with colleagues will support your own professional learning and resilience. This section introduces key ideas in workplace learning, focused on identifying and becoming an active member of 'learning communities' at a range of levels, from finding a colleague willing to be an informal buddy, to being a member of an effective teaching team, to collaboration with colleagues and parents, to contributing as a member of a wider teacher network.

Schools as learning organisations

This book is aimed at you as an individual teacher, but you need to work within your workplace, involving a teaching team and an organisation. As a professional teacher your role is not merely to experience that workplace: you may also help to shape it. Even as a trainee or newly qualified teacher you will be having an impact on the culture and ways of working in the organisation, no matter how insignificant you might feel.

Every organisation may be considered to have a 'learning architecture' which provides affordances for workplace learning (Billet, 2004). This architecture will include deliberately designed formal support structures such as designated departments, teams and line managers. But also very importantly the workplace will include informal learning structures and opportunities that may be nurtured but cannot be imposed by managers. These informal workplace learning elements may include one-to-one chats with a critical friend during coffee breaks, informal groups of teachers who share their practice during breaks or after school, and effective relationships with teaching assistants that allow provision of feedback from observations during lessons. There are considerable assumptions and power relationships underlying the concept of the learning organisation, and in critically evaluating its usefulness we might well ask: 'Who is the learning organisation for?'

In the literature there is strong support for knowledge-based organisations such as a school, where a large proportion of the budget is spent on paying the teaching staff, to invest heavily in creating a positive learning environment for those staff. However, there is a balance to be struck between a high-accountability managerialist regime and a more collegial and flexible culture with a relatively flat hierarchy in terms of management. School leaders may be seen as having a mediating role, as they have to filter and control the impact of external pressures on their teachers and learners.

As a beginning teacher you may find yourself working in a formal team, with a designated line manager, and perhaps also a formal workplace mentor. As we suggested in this chapter's introduction, it is wise to find yourself a critical friend: an informal buddy. You will ideally build sufficient trust to work effectively and honestly with your line manager. However, having an additional critical friend adds another important means of support, which offers something different from formal management structures. The workplace culture of the school and the disposition and skills of individual colleagues in these roles will strongly influence how much you learn from these more formal arrangements and how supported they make you feel.

A useful framework for evaluating your setting is the expansive–restrictive workplace learning environment continuum, which was initially developed from studies of a range of commercial and industrial workplaces but has been applied to schools (Hodkinson and Hodkinson, 2005).

You might consider, for each characteristic in the framework in Table 6.2, where on the continuum between expansive and restrictive your current workplace seems to sit. What are its strengths and weaknesses in terms of its workplace learning architecture? An additional characteristic, perhaps missing from the framework in Table 6.2, is 'shared purpose'. To what extent do you feel that your team in your current workplace has a clear and explicit shared purpose: a common aim?

Based on Table 6.2 you may feel that you are fortunate and have a generally expansive workplace that supports your professional learning. On the other hand you may feel frustrated if your current workplace is towards the restrictive end of the continuum on many of the characteristics. In either situation the framework in Table 6.2 may help you to identify opportunities for being proactive and shifting your workplace at least slightly towards the expansive end of the continuum. Perhaps the obvious first step is to identify and approach a possible informal mentor or critical friend. By developing a sense of identity and ambition,

Table 6.2 The expansive–restrictive workplace learning environment continuum for teachers

Expansive	Restrictive
Close collaborative working	Isolated, individualist working
Colleagues mutually supportive in enhancing teacher learning	Colleagues obstruct or do not support each other's learning
An explicit focus on teacher learning, as a dimension of normal working practices	No explicit focus on teacher learning, except to meet crises or imposed initiatives
Supported opportunities for personal development that goes beyond school or government priorities	Teacher learning mainly involves strategic compliance with government or school agendas
Out-of-school educational opportunities, including time to stand back, reflect and think differently	Few out-of-school educational opportunities, only narrow, short training programmes
Opportunities to integrate off-the-job learning into everyday practice	No opportunity to integrate off-the-job learning
Opportunities to participate in more than one working group	Work restricted to home departmental teams within one school
Opportunity to extend professional identity through boundary crossing into other departments, school activities, schools and beyond	Opportunities for boundary crossing only come with a job change
Support for local variation in ways of working and learning for teachers and work groups	Standardised approaches to teacher learning are prescribed and imposed
Teachers use a wide range of learning opportunities	Teachers use a narrow range of learning approaches

Hodkinson, H. & Hodkinson, P. (2005) Improving schoolteachers' workplace learning. *Research Papers in Education*, 20(2), 109–131, p 124, reproduced by permission of Taylor & Francis.

by acting with integrity and by collaborating within an ethical code, we can help to make our workplaces more expansive and take charge of our professional learning as teachers. Even in the most restrictive workplaces it will normally be possible to form some kind of informal network to support you in your work and to help you to continue to learn.

Some teachers will claim that they are too busy to concern themselves with their own learning and must prioritise the needs of their learners. However, we would argue that managing your development is a professional responsibility and is for the benefit of your learners. In the short term a learning teacher is a happier teacher and in the medium term you need to continue to develop, for example, in response to changing policy, technology and research evidence, in order to remain effective for your learners.

Some school leaders argue strongly that external accountability, for example, inspection reports and published league tables of school test results, must set the agenda for professional development for teachers. Clearly, these will be a significant influence, but the school needs to develop a clearer and broader mission for the education it wishes to provide, and ensure that its professional development for teachers is aligned with that purpose.

Learning communities

As a teacher you may be fortunate to be working closely with a group of colleagues with a shared sense of purpose and collaboratively developed tools and ways of working, for example, including a set of teaching strategies that are considered to be effective in your school. This situation may be described as a 'community of practice' (Wenger, 1998). It is important to note that a formally designated department or team may or may not operate as a community of practice. Membership of a community of practice is voluntary and is gained through learning the shared ways of working, participating and then contributing to help shape the community. As a teacher you may become a member of more than one community of practice and in some cases these might extend beyond your workplace setting.

As you negotiate your membership of teacher communities of practice you will need to appreciate the history of the group and of individual members and the unwritten values and rules that apply. You will need to appreciate the relationships within the group and the status claimed by some members, perhaps as a result of their long membership or specialist knowledge. You are likely to require some measure of resilience as your attempts to join the group are variously welcomed or possibly resisted by existing members or by members of alternative communities within the school.

The idea of teachers forming 'learning communities' has a long history (Cochran-Smith and Lytle, 1999; Hargreaves and Fullan, 2012), but unfortunately the term has often been used rather flexibly and without taking into account the context of schools as workplaces. The members of a 'community of practice' develop a shared purpose and goals. It may be desirable but not always easy for a formal structure in a school such as a department of teachers to become a 'learning community' with the characteristics of a community of practice (Skerrett, 2010). There may be contradictions within the workplace as a learning organisation, tensions that prevent the required levels of collaboration and trust to develop. For example, if school leaders are quick to make judgements on the quality of teaching by individuals, then it would not be surprising if teachers were cautious about making a video of one of their lessons and sharing their practice with others. However, if teachers are proactive and collaborative, then these kinds of tensions may even provide a useful driver for professional learning and for expansive learning that helps to shift thinking and ways of working within the workplace (Levine, 2010).

The overlapping communities or networks that you might experience or seek to develop may include: a formal teaching team or department in your school; a less formal group of colleagues in school that you find you can relate to and tend to share and collaborate with; an informal mentor teacher you use occasionally for informal support, who might work in your school or elsewhere; some teachers with a similar role in other partnership schools; a subject specialist network of teachers (for example, the Geography Association or the Association for Science Education); one or two colleagues that you trained with and keep in touch with; a group of teachers that are completing a part-time masters programme with you, and so on. These examples range from networks both within and external to your school and from more formal professional arrangements to more informal social contacts. Some networks will be face-to-face and others will be blended or fully online. You will need to be personally proactive in developing such networks as they will support your professional learning and career development. If you fail to get promotion or a particular post in the future, it is no good reflecting back and blaming the headteacher or the school for not providing sufficient opportunities or training. Much professional learning is informal and can be pursued whatever your work situation; even formal professional development programmes requiring fees will mainly be of value to the extent that they support and provoke your workplace learning.

Increasingly, there are useful blogs, online forums and social media networks that you may turn to for sharing ideas, reading about innovative practice, engaging with research evidence and generally chatting about the joys and challenges of teaching. There are some great blogs and useful websites, but the normal unwritten rules of using online social networks apply and with an extra point that your professional reputation is at stake. There are commercial interests in the education sector as well as individuals with different levels of expertise. It is easy to use precious time engaging online, and you will need to experiment and consider the benefits. However, it is certainly worth engaging with online resources to get an introduction to an issue or strategy, and in many cases you will find opportunities to network with other teachers alongside open access materials on any particular classroom or school issue. At times there is a kind of frenzy that drives a good deal of social media: a desire to be up to date and to deal with the latest emerging ideas. As a teacher you face considerable challenges affecting social justice, and your professional practice should not be simply reduced to a series of choices around strategies for classroom teaching.

Thinking reflectively on your current networks, to what extent do you feel you are a member, or at least a peripheral member, of a key learning community within your workplace? To what extent are you gaining full membership through increasing collaboration and contribution? What appears to be the shared purpose of the community and what are the unwritten rules? You might also reflect on other communities or networks that you currently belong to and how you might strengthen your membership of those and build stronger working relationships with other members. Do you collaborate in any way across boundaries, for example, with teachers in a different team within your workplace?

As a beginning teacher you may feel you have only provisional membership of a small number of professional learning communities. But during your career you are likely to develop membership of a number of both formal and informal learning communities, and if you are fortunate or proactively persistent then these may overlap considerably. It is important that you are proactive in becoming an active member of learning communities and in initiating or developing them as required.

Things to try

» *Identify a critical friend on the staff of your current school and talk to her about a classroom issue you are currently working on. Perhaps set up a reciprocal arrangement where you will talk to each other over a given period about an issue that is troubling both of you. We are all pushed for time, but this can be quite low-key. Thousands of these conversations take place in an ad hoc way every day in schools, and those chats over a coffee can be very useful indeed, so this is just a way to formalise that slightly, but without making it onerous.*

» *Evaluate your school or department on the expansive–restrictive workplace learning environment continuum and consider what actions you could take to start to shape it to be more expansive. Every little helps, so it doesn't have to be a major initiative. For example, you might be able to initiate some collaborative planning with other teachers in a curriculum area in which you have some expertise.*

» *Review your current membership of teacher learning communities and consider practical steps you might take in joining or strengthening internal and external networks. This could be in-school working parties; local groups involving teachers in other schools; following carefully selected blogs; being part of online networks. We recommend being a proactive member of a teachers' curriculum subject association for your area of specialism.*

» *Invite a critical friend into one of your lessons informally to observe your learners and give an additional perspective on an issue you are focusing on. Make a reciprocal offer. Find some time afterwards to have a chat about what you both think was going on in the lesson; for example, ask a critical friend, 'Could you pop into the last 20 minutes of my Maths lesson on Tuesday? I'm doing some group work and I'm not quite sure I'm getting the most out of it – would you come and help me have a think about it?' This kind of informal but focused collaboration can be very useful.*

Reflections on Sammie's science lesson

Before reading on it is worth pausing now to reflect critically on Sammie's lesson, presented at the beginning of this chapter. Considering the key ideas on collaboration for learning, how might we evaluate Sammie's lesson and what next steps should he take? In the following discussion section we set out our general perspective, but it is more important that you consider Sammie's lesson in relation to your own practice in your current workplace.

1. **What was the purpose of the group work? Did each person in the group feel they had a shared purpose, and that they would be individually accountable for their contribution? Is the group task any more than a presentation? Would a learner who had designed an attractive title for the group poster think that he had succeeded in this group task? Did group work strengthen the progress of learners during the lesson?**

In becoming a scientist, a fundamental concept must be to understand ways of knowing in science, generally meaning the nature of the scientific method in terms of a fair test or experiment. Whatever the particular choice of experiment (and that will be affected by what equipment or materials are available), Sammie could have designed this particular lesson with the key idea of scientific method more firmly at its heart. Sammie chose a low-risk approach in more ways than one. By controlling the experiment, at best allowing selected children to help out, Sammie appears to be keeping the physical risk of hot water scalding to a minimum. But what about the risk of predicting, of setting out hypotheses for each part of the experiment? This might easily have been delegated to the groups and been part of their poster presentation. In making the test 'fair' it may also have been possible to involve the groups in coming up with ideas. For example, they may have proposed the idea of keeping each sample of material a similar volume or mass, or of leaving it in the hot water for a similar time.

In Sammie's approach to the lesson the group work does appear to have some value in terms of provoking a learning conversation, though there is little guidance on what this conversation might entail. However, by using grouping by ability and by assigning a group leader Sammie may not have maximised the opportunities for dialogue within the groups. We must also bear in mind that the assessment data Sammie uses to formulate the groups are based on literacy and numeracy tracking. This raises all sorts of other questions about the assumptions that are being made about the children and how they may respond to this task. The task does seem to be low-challenge and mainly about the presentation of the findings of a teacher-led experiment. Sammie also seems to have a clear idea of what the posters should look like and does not even allow much scope for the groups in terms of creativity in presenting the findings. Even if working as a group member was a key learning outcome for the lesson, there does not seem to have been any explicit expectations or teaching of group skills and a lack of any review of how effectively the group collaborated. In this sense, then, the group work was rather superficial and has probably not made a significant contribution to the progress of the learners.

We talked earlier about learning being an act of 'deliberate co-construction', but there seems to be little of this going on here, and there is potential for Sammie to increase the learning substantially by rethinking the collaborative element. Sammie has ticked a box allowing him to think that he has tackled group work (which he was a little nervous about), so in terms of building Sammie's confidence in organising this sort of lesson, he has reason to be pleased. However, to his credit he realises that the level of learning is more questionable. It is perfectly possible that the children may leave this lesson feeling they had worked hard, that they'd been on task and even that they'd enjoyed themselves. Some of them (perhaps the ones responsible for producing the attractive posters) may be especially pleased with their output. However, the learning at the heart of the lesson does not seem to be as secure as it could have been.

2. We know that some of the learners really enjoyed the activities in the lesson. How should the teacher balance this enjoyment in evaluating the effectiveness of the lesson?

Feedback from learners is useful but it must always be analysed thoughtfully. Engagement of learners is a key element of successful teaching, typically observed in a classroom perhaps by a low hum of conversation, a high level of on-task activity and good quality work produced by all. However, this last point is critical: was there a sufficiently high level of challenge so that all learners were engaged in work at or beyond their current level of ability? Did some learners essentially fail to complete the task fully but still demonstrate progress in learning? If learners are 'enjoying' your lessons then that has to be a good thing, but are they enjoying them because they make for easy success? Are they enjoying taking part in activities which are not central to the learning (in this case, designing attractive posters)? Sammie's lesson was very much teacher-led and low risk in terms of any kind of uncertain outcome. Positive feedback for such a lesson seems more likely to come from compliant rather than autonomous learners and more likely to come from learners with a fixed than a growth mindset. Of course, we want children to enjoy our lessons, but we need them to enjoy them for the right reasons.

3. Do these children know how to work together in groups? Have the expectations of group interaction been made clear? Do the children think it matters how they work together in the group? Were they directed to review their group work in any way?

If Sammie had been able to increase the complexity and risks involved in the task then it might have provided a suitable challenge for the groups of learners. Consider, however, how it might have been possible to set out some expectations for collaborative learning and working in a group. Even if the learners are familiar with group work, it is still worth reminding them, for example, about negotiating roles, active listening, giving and receiving feedback and turn-taking. As part of the lesson plenary it is important to find time for learners to self-assess their contribution to the group task. Sammie allowed the class to work right up to the lesson end in order to get as much completion as possible of the posters. It is more important to stop with sufficient time to complete a plenary, including a metacognitive element asking 'How did we learn today?' Admittedly, it is early days for Sammie and he can build on the boost in confidence this lesson has given him in terms of his ability to organise the logistics of group work. He may feel he is pushed for time and can't invest time in talking about how to approach group work as well as how to respond to the experiment. However, this investment will reward Sammie and the children much more richly in the long run and can form part of his ongoing work with this class.

4. Does the teacher seem to make the best use of the support provided by the teaching assistant? If the teaching assistant had been off sick that day, then how might that have affected the impact of grouping the learners? Is ability grouping a good idea?

In a busy school day it is not always easy to brief teaching assistants fully, but it is important if they are to play a full part in supporting learning. In Sammie's lesson grouping by some measure of current ability may have been done simply because 'That's how we do it in this school'. It also makes the delegation of work to the teaching assistant apparently simpler by their allocation to the 'low-ability' group. This seems easier than asking the teaching assistant to work across mixed-ability groups but may actually reinforce low expectations of the group and of the teaching assistant.

Sammie also mentions producing a more structured worksheet for the 'lower-ability' groups. This kind of differentiation by task is time-consuming for the teacher and in some cultural contexts, for example in France, would be seen as risking embedding differences within the group of learners (Raveaud, 2005). Mixed-ability or other heterogeneous (mixed) groups would get rid of the need for differentiation by task and help to encourage dialogue between learners by setting a high-challenge task with a shared purpose.

5.   To what extent does Sammie seem to be collaborating with the teacher mentor? How might this relationship be developed by Sammie to become more productive in terms of professional learning?

Sammie is doing his best to respond to the teacher mentor's suggestions for the lesson, which seem a very well-meaning attempt to help Sammie develop his skills. It can be difficult to disagree with suggestions established staff make, particularly when you are in training or newly qualified. When these suggestions are part of well-established school practices, resisting them in any way is made even more tricky.

The mentor's suggestion that Sammie steps things up a bit makes Sammie nervous, but this seems to be a good opportunity for this beginning teacher and his mentor to collaborate more closely. Sammie should feel that he can draw on his mentor's support to develop the use of group work. We have previously emphasised the fact that many established teaching staff are open to new approaches, and learning from new entrants to the profession, as well as from established colleagues, is something many experienced staff welcome. Sammie should be able to work within the guidance given by the mentor, but feel he can also contribute something to the discussion.

In deciding to go ahead and experiment with group work, Sammie could also perhaps have asked the teaching assistant to provide observation feedback on its impact on learning. Involving the learners in a meta-review of the group work would also provide useful data to become part of the overall evaluation, and this would help Sammie's own learning. Adopting this kind of inquiry-based approach in collaboration with colleagues would help Sammie to enjoy learning, feel more supported and help to shape the workplace by increasing the number of conversations about teaching and learning.

Things to try

Reflecting on Sammie's lesson, consider one of your own lesson plans. Consider how you too could adopt some of the principles of Bennett et al's (2005) characteristics of effective group work identified earlier in this chapter and invoked in the commentary on Sammie's lesson, above. Adapt your design to maximise collaborative learning. Teach the revised lesson and ask the question: 'What is my impact on learning and learners?' You might ask some of these questions:

» *What is the purpose of the group work? How does this support the intended learning for the lesson? Is each person in the group accountable for their actions within the group?*

» *How can you understand best the learners' response to the lesson? How will you gauge how they have responded to the group work?*

» *Do your learners understand how to work together in the group? Do you need to spend time teaching them about working in a group?*

» *Organise your class into mixed-ability groups, or, better still, mixed groups that don't privilege the concept of 'ability'. How do you feel this has an impact on learning and on the learners? If possible, ask a critical friend or formal mentor to observe the group work element of the lesson and help you think about its impact.*

Chapter 6 summary

This chapter provides an overview of the merits of creating opportunities for learners to work collaboratively with each other and on a regular basis. This requires learners to see learning in an expansive and generous light, rather than something that has to be rationed and parcelled out.

Learning power

• Well-designed and facilitated co-operative working, with group goals and individual accountability for contribution, has powerful learning outcomes.

• Learning is promoted by activities and classroom cultures that encourage dialogue, with opportunities for sharing ideas and giving and receiving feedback.

• An explicit focus on social skills for group work and on review of group work is important.

• To develop high challenge for all learners it is possible to used mixed groups, and grouping by some measure of current level of performance does not in itself ensure effective collaborative learning.

Teachers' workplace learning

• Your workplace, within a learning organisation, may be positioned for different characteristics of the learning environment along the continuum between expansive and restrictive.

• While you may have limited power it is always possible to take small steps to shape your workplace learning environment and to build relevant and supportive networks beyond your institution: finding a buddy or critical friend is a first step.

• Achieving full membership of a learning community requires you to learn the rules and participate, but also to contribute, so that you are helping to shape the community, including its purpose and its ways of working.

Taking it further

- A useful and concise introduction to collaborative working and learning in the classroom is Luzet (2013).

- Mercer (2000) is a well-argued guide for teachers on the development of dialogue and its significance for learning. It has plenty of examples of interactions and practical strategies.

- Although aimed at lead practitioners in early years and primary schools, DCSF (2008) is a useful open access online resource with plenty of practical ideas for developing dialogue and sustained shared thinking in your classroom.

References

Alexander, R. (2004) *Towards Dialogic Teaching: Rethinking Classroom Talk*. York: Dialogos.

Bennett, J., Lubben, F., Hogarth, S., Campbell, B. and Robinson, A. (2005) *A Systematic Review of the Nature of Small-Group Discussions Aimed at Improving Students' Understanding of Evidence in Science*. London: EPPI-Centre, Social Science Research Unit, Institute of Education, University of London.

Billett, S. (2004) Co-Participation at Work: Learning through Work and throughout Working Lives. *Studies in the Education of Adults*, 36(2), pp 190–205.

Buber, M. (1958) *I and Thou* (trans. R. Gregor Smith). Edinburgh: T&T Clark.

Cochran-Smith, M. and Lytle, S. L. (1999) Relationships of Knowledge and Practice: Teacher Learning in Communities. *Review of Research in Education*, 24, pp 249–73.

DCSF (Department for Children, Schools and Families) (2008) *Every Child a Talker: Guidance for Lead Practitioners*. London: DCSF. Available at: http://webarchive.nationalarchives.gov.uk/20130401151715/https://www.education.gov.uk/publications/eOrderingDownload/DCSF-00854-2008.pdf (accessed 1 May 2015).

Hargreaves, A. and Fullan, M. (2012) *Professional Capital: Transforming Teaching in Every School*. New York: Teachers College Press.

Hattie, J. (2009) *Visible Learning: A Synthesis of over 800 Meta-Analyses Relating to Achievement*. Abingdon: Routledge.

Hattie, J. (2012) *Visible Learning for Teachers: Maximising Impact on Learning*. Abingdon: Routledge.

Higgins, S., Kokotsaki, D. and Coe, R. (2011) *Toolkit of Strategies to Improve Learning: Summary for Schools Spending the Pupil Premium*. Durham: CEM and Durham University.

Hodkinson, H. and Hodkinson, P. (2005) Improving Schoolteachers' Workplace Learning. *Research Papers in Education*, 20(2), pp 109–31.

Johnson, D. W. and Johnson, R. T. (1999) *Learning Together and Alone: Cooperative, Competitive and Individualistic Learning*. Boston: Allyn & Bacon.

Johnson, D. W., Maruyama, G., Johnson, R. T., Nelson, D. and Skon, R. (1981) Effects of Cooperative, Competitive and Individualistic Goal Structures on Achievement: A Meta-Analysis. *Psychological Bulletin*, 89(1), pp 47–62.

Levine, T. H. (2010) Tools for the Study and Design of Collaborative Teacher Learning: The Affordances of Different Conceptions of Teacher Community and Activity. *Teacher Education Quarterly*, 37, pp 109–21.

Lipsey, M. W. and Wilson, D. B. (1993) The Efficacy of Psychological, Educational and Behavioural Treatment: Confirmation from Meta-Analysis. *American Psychologist*, 48(12), pp 1181–209.

Luzet, G. (2013) *Collaborative Learning Pocketbook*. Alresford: Teachers' Pocketbooks.

Marzano, R. J., Norford, J. S., Paynter, D. E., Pickering, D. J. and Gaddy, B. B. (2001) *A Handbook for Classroom Instruction That Works*. Alexandria, VA: Association for Supervision and Curriculum Development.

Mercer, N. (2000) *Words and Minds: How We Use Language to Think Together*. London: Routledge.

Raveaud, M. (2005) Hares, Tortoises and the Social Construction of the Pupil: Differentiated Learning in French and English Primary Schools. *British Educational Research Journal*, 31(4), pp 459–79.

Roseth, C. J., Fang, F., Johnson, D. W. and Johnson, R. T. (2006) Effects of Cooperative Learning on Middle School Students: A Meta-Analysis. Presented at *American Educational Research Association Conference*, San Francisco, CA, April, 2006.

Rui, N. (2009) Four Decades of Research on the Effects of Detracking Reform: Where Do We Stand? A Systematic Review of the Evidence. *Journal of Evidence-Based Medicine*, 2(3), pp 164–83.

Skerrett, A. (2010) 'There's Going to be Community. There's Going to be Knowledge': Designs for Learning in a Standardized Age. *Teaching and Teacher Education*, 26, pp 648–55.

Stenhouse, L. (1967) *Culture and Education*. London: Nelson.

Stenhouse, L. (1975) *An Introduction to Curriculum Research and Development*. London: Heinemann.

Sylva, K., Melhuish, E., Sammons, P., Siraj-Blatchford, I. and Taggart, B. (2004) *The Effective Provision of Pre-School Education (EPPE) Project: Final Report*. London: DfES. Available at: http://webarchive.nationalarchives.gov.uk/20090617172700/http:/dcsf.gov.uk/everychildmatters/publications/0/1160/ (accessed 12 April 2015).

Vygotsky, L. S. (1978) *Mind in Society*. Cambridge, MA: Harvard University Press.

Walberg, H. J. (1999) Productive Teaching. In H. C. Waxman and H. J. Walberg (eds) *New Directions for Teaching Practice and Research*. Berkeley, CA: McCutchan, pp 75–104.

Watkins, C. (2005) *Classrooms as Learning Communities: What's In It for Schools?* Abingdon: Routledge.

Wenger, E. (1998) *Communities of Practice: Learning, Meaning, and Identity*. Cambridge: Cambridge University Press.

Chapter 7 Epilogue: getting it all together

Whether you've been reading this book assiduously, sequentially and seriously, or dipping into it sporadically, erratically and whimsically, thank you for getting to this point. We hope you've been challenged, enlightened, perplexed, intrigued and even a little bemused at times. If so, you've captured something of the various experiences you'll have as a teacher over the next 30 years or so.

In this final section we

- **recap the key messages of this book for you;**
- **map the teacher dilemmas to more traditional key areas of teacher knowledge and practice;**
- **offer some brief advice on your career development in education;**
- **challenge you to put into action some of the ideas arising from the five core chapters.**

Key messages

This book is aimed at new teachers but is part of a wider body of literature aimed at educators, school leaders, parents and policy-makers that builds on the idea of malleable intelligence. The concept of growth mindset is fundamental to our view of becoming an inspirational teacher. As a teacher with a growth mindset in relation to your own professional learning, you will know that through effort, practice and reflection on your practice (especially your mistakes) you are capable of becoming an inspirational teacher.

Even more importantly, you believe that all of your learners are capable of becoming smarter through effort and deep practice as they struggle with the high-challenge learning activities that you have skilfully designed and facilitated. You know that your responsibility as a teacher includes setting high expectations based on your own beliefs on malleable intelligence, nurturing growth mindsets in your learners and including a focus on thinking dispositions. In this way we argue that you can gain engagement and good test results for your learners in response to the high-accountability context of your work, but also develop your learners as self-regulated, lifelong learners.

This book is also part of the wider body of literature on the development of research-informed practice in schools. The metaphor for teachers' professional learning as interplay between practical wisdom and public knowledge is fundamental to our view of becoming an inspirational teacher. We argue that teachers must continue to be learners themselves through inquiry-based, sustained, collaborative professional development activity that includes critical engagement with public knowledge. Your learners deserve research-informed practice and that means you need to pursue interplay between the vertical domain of public (published) knowledge and the horizontal domain of practical wisdom, as illustrated by Figure 7.1. Though we welcome the insights that large-scale quantitative research and research meta-reviews provide, we argue that extracting from these top-down, simplistic prescriptive notions of how to teach is a recipe for failure. Knowledge creation in teaching requires full engagement of professional teachers rather than some kind of curriculum delivery by technicians. You might consider your agency as a professional teacher to be a third dimension, piercing the heart of the metaphorical framework shown in Figure 7.1. You also need to be aware that

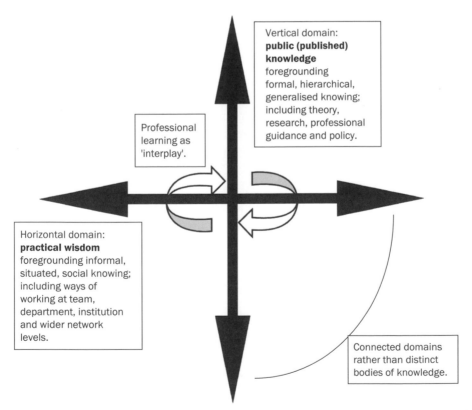

Figure 7.1 *Teacher professional learning as 'interplay' between practical wisdom and public knowledge (Boyd, 2014; Boyd and Bloxham, 2014)*

horizontal practical wisdom will vary from one school to another as you move through your career. Finally, you will appreciate that the vertical domain includes a complex interweaving of curriculum subject knowledge, of knowledge of schooling within its wider context and of pedagogy, with its multiple paradigms and contested evidence base.

In the core chapters of this book we have therefore not offered oven-ready 'how to teach' guides. Rather, we've offered challenging dilemmas facing you as a teacher. We propose that you engage with these dilemmas through collaborative, sustained, inquiry-based approaches that include critical engagement with public knowledge and classroom experimentation and evaluation. We encourage you to become a self-regulated teacher-learner by pursuing ongoing practitioner research projects. We mentioned at the start of this book that basic well-planned teaching is central to your practice. Good-quality teacher explanations followed by increasingly independent practice by learners and accompanied by feedback should be a key element of your portfolio of teacher strategies. However, we would add that learners are able to develop expertise in the curriculum subject disciplines by engaging with key concepts, frameworks and ways of knowing at an early stage, and that this is essential in order to engage them sufficiently as they gradually build relevant factual knowledge. The experience of 'becoming' a scientist, geographer, historian, mathematician and so on is part of learning at an early stage and should not be reserved for university or postgraduate level education, as some would have it. The challenge for you as a teacher is that you need to develop high-level understanding of key concepts, frameworks and epistemology (ways of knowing) in the curriculum subject disciplines that you teach.

Mapping the teacher dilemmas to traditional areas of practice

This book has adopted an unconventional approach by building the core chapters around teacher dilemmas. It therefore seems worthwhile to map the dilemmas to more traditional key areas of practice that you are likely to find in the structure of standard 'how to teach' texts and in the relevant professional standards for teaching that you are working within. The idea is to help you to relate your learning from this book to more conventional professional guidance and standards frameworks for teacher practice and to education policy that affects you at national and school level (see Table 7.1).

Further study and inquiry

As we established at the start of this book, we do not attempt to 'cover' all of the complexity of becoming a teacher. On balance, we have probably provided more questions than answers. The 'Taking it further' prompts in each core chapter provide some guidance for wider reading to support your further classroom experimentation and inquiry. As part of your continuing professional learning we recommend that you also buy a standard teacher education text relevant to your particular context and to the professional standards that you need to address. Further study is also recommended in four particular areas that are not addressed fully within this book; these areas are briefly noted after Table 7.1, which illustrates the traditional areas of practice covered in this book.

Table 7.1 Traditional areas of teacher practice and the sections of this book that are relevant

Traditional area of practice	Relevant sections of this book
Planning and subject knowledge content	This important area of teachers' work is most explicitly discussed in Chapter 4, 'Abstract versus concrete'. We argue that classroom activities should allow learners to approach key concepts and ways of knowing within the subject discipline so that they are 'becoming' a scientist, historian and so on. We adopt a realistic approach to your development of curriculum content knowledge: it will take years of experience to refine it, but we do emphasise the urgent need for you to understand the key concepts underpinning your lessons. Planning is about challenge and progression and some aspects of this are addressed by Chapter 2, 'Belief versus ability'.
Equality, diversity and inclusion	These important issues are partially considered in relation to collaborating with parents in Chapter 5, 'Feedback versus praise'. Also, we believe that focusing on thinking dispositions has a social justice dimension and hope that throughout the book we have demonstrated our own commitment to equality and diversity. However, we acknowledge that the book does not explicitly address the considerable challenges for teachers and schools in this area and we recommend further investigation.
Teaching	The book argues for an orchestration by the teacher of important curriculum content with learning to learn – as seen in current debates around teaching the formal curriculum and teaching 'character'. That is why our key question for teachers is phrased as 'What is my impact on learning and learners?' Learning to learn through metacognition and meta-learning is particularly addressed in Chapter 2, 'Belief versus ability'. Curriculum subject content knowledge is addressed by Chapter 4, 'Abstract versus concrete'. Chapter 6, 'Collaboration versus competition', covers important ideas about designing learning activities and organising your classroom environment to maximise learning.
Assessment	The learning power of formative assessment is most explicitly considered in Chapter 5, 'Feedback versus praise'. However, throughout the book, including Chapter 2, 'Belief versus ability', we have discussed the related issues of designing high-challenge open-ended tasks, setting high expectations and creating a learning environment where mistakes and failure are seen as opportunities for learning through formative assessment.
Managing your own learning	The 'workplace learning sections' from Chapter 2 to Chapter 6 provide an overview and suggested school-based activities to help you become more proactive in managing your continuing professional development.
Developing your professional values and beliefs	Chapter 2, 'Belief versus ability', introduces teacher identity, and this is where we particularly encourage you to develop an ambitious sense of mission or purpose for your contribution to the teaching profession and to the wider field of education. This is partly related to your values around achieving excellence for yourself and your learners as well as issues of equality, diversity and inclusion.

1.   Within this book we have introduced the approach of focusing on your impact on learning and also on learners. This second element means integrating a focus on thinking dispositions within your lessons. We recommend further study and inquiry on the development of growth mindsets and thinking dispositions.

2.   This book reflects our belief that focusing on development of thinking dispositions in your learners will contribute towards social justice aims in education. However, part of being an effective teacher is to understand your learners, to be able to empathise with them and to provide relevant support. We therefore recommend further study and inquiry on learning needs, inclusion, diversity, equality and social justice.

3.   We have deliberately used fairly traditional mainstream lessons and learning activities in our five classroom scenarios so that many teachers in a range of settings will be able to identify with them. This is not intended to place any limits on your creativity as a teacher or to suppress your engagement with technology to support learning in your classroom. We recommend further study and classroom inquiry on the role of information technology in learning.

4.   We have proposed teacher inquiry and practitioner research as a powerful framework for leading change in practice. However, there is a wider literature on leading change in schools and on school improvement that is certainly worth engaging with. We consider that all teachers should position themselves as leaders within a distributed leadership framework. This leadership role is part of being a professional teacher, rather than merely a technician 'delivering' the curriculum. We recommend further study and inquiry on leading change and school leadership.

It may seem unfair as you approach the end of this book for the authors to set out further areas for reading and inquiry. Of course, we recommend that you use this book to prompt your classroom experimentation and inquiry over a period of time. However, becoming an inspirational teacher requires continued professional learning, and that learning requires interplay between public knowledge and the practical wisdom evident in your practice and in the ways of working of other expert teachers in your school. It is important that you continually seek external public knowledge and critically consider its relevance for improving learning in your context.

Your development as a teacher

As we move towards the end of this book you might be forgiven for feeling that as a beginning teacher it is relentlessly asking you for more: more planning, more creativity, more evaluation and especially more time for your own professional learning. You are probably working too hard already and may reasonably ask where this additional effort and time is to come from. There is no doubt that becoming an inspirational teacher is not an easy path. Teachers who have taken this path in the past testify to this in the titles of books they've written about their experiences – for example, *There Are No Shortcuts* (Esquith, 2003) – and you will require considerable resilience. We recommend that you clarify your mission, a written statement setting out your successes, core values, short-term goals, the long-term contribution you wish to make and the kind of teacher you want to become. Then it is possible to plan your time each working week to include at least one session of 'mission-critical' activity which helps you to work towards your ambitions (Covey, 2004). It may often be possible to integrate the everyday work you need to get done with an element of professional learning. For example, when grading some student work you might be experimenting with a revised form of written feedback and evaluating the impact of the teaching strategy used in the previous lessons. You should develop habits of 'working smart', including:

*   avoid procrastination (identify a first step towards the task and do it);

*   use the 'four ds' for mail and email (do it, diarise it, delegate it or ditch it);

*   prioritise (use lists and a 'tnt' note – the next thing – whenever you leave your work);

*   learn to say no ('Thank you for considering me but I currently have other priorities');

*   be present 'in the moment' for family and friends (plan for time off work).

Despite such strategies, the biggest challenge for you as a teacher is likely to be finding time for meaningful collaboration with other teachers. This must be a priority for you because it is potentially so powerful for your professional learning.

Professional capital

The process of building your capacity as you become an inspirational teacher will take several years and has been captured in a useful way by the concept of 'professional capital' (Hargreaves and Fullan, 2012, p 78). Andy Hargreaves and Michael Fullan argue that teachers' professional capital, their capacity to help all their students learn and thrive, is a function of human capital (HC), social capital (SC) and decisional capital (DC) and may be expressed in the formula:

$$Professional\ Capital = f(HC, SC, DC).$$

The human capital of a teacher includes their knowledge and skills, including knowledge of subject, of pedagogy and of children. It is also about the emotional capabilities and commitment to support diverse learners as well as other adults involved. Social capital is about trusting professional relationships and interactions that give you access as a teacher to the human capital of others. Building your social capital includes finding a critical friend and collaborating with other teachers in your inquiry projects. Decisional capital is built through your deliberative practice as a teacher, so that through multiple decisions in the classroom and around the school you are gradually becoming an expert. There is no shortcut to building decisional capital, but the level of discretion and scope for experimentation in your workplace will be an important factor. Hargreaves and Fullan (2012) successfully develop and position the concept of professional capital at the heart of the international drive for education improvement and that is a movement that you will wish to contribute to as a professional teacher.

Career development

A large-scale study of teachers in the UK suggested that their highest levels of effectiveness were between 8 and 23 years in the job (Day et al, 2007; Hargreaves and Fullan, 2012, p 70). This suggests that as a beginning teacher you have access to a grace period during which you can legitimately focus on professional development and enjoy becoming more expert without getting too frustrated by mistakes you make along the way. We suggest that you consider your induction as a teacher to be a period of three to five years. Many new teachers will shine early, and through useful skills in behaviour management and positive relationships with learners may appear to be highly competent. This does not mean that they do not deserve and need continuing professional development. Perhaps controversially, we would recommend that you are cautious about accepting early promotion, because leadership roles may distract you from developing your knowledge and skills as a classroom practitioner. Above all, you need to surround yourself with a network of committed, professional teachers who will support your professional learning. Having suggested that you avoid early promotion, we do, however, suggest that you experiment with early 'stealth' leadership by developing inquiry-based projects and recruiting colleagues to collaborate with you. Leading change through a bottom-up approach will help you to develop powerful values and skills for distributed leadership and prepare you for formal roles in the future.

What next?

This book views effective teaching as an orchestration of beliefs, strategies and relationships that shapes a complex social situation rather than a series of distinct interventions such as formative assessment, metacognition, mastery learning and collaborative working. For this reason, meta-reviews of research are useful indicators of what works, but they are strictly limited in their value for telling leaders and teachers in a particular school what to do next. For that we need to rely on professional learning and wise judgement gained through interplay between vertical public knowledge and horizontal practical wisdom. We propose that such interplay can be achieved through sustained, collaborative inquiry in which, as a teacher, you continually ask the question:

- *What is my impact on learning and learners?*

Pursue this through increasingly sophisticated and collaborative approaches, including ongoing systematic inquiry and practitioner research projects.

Taking it further

Hargreaves, A. and Fullan, M. (2012) *Professional Capital: Transforming Teaching in Every School.* New York: Teachers College Press.

This is a well-argued and inspiring book that provides a convincing review of education development internationally and offers the concept of professional capital as a way to capture the development of teaching as a profession.

Hattie, J. (2012) *Visible Learning for Teachers: Maximizing Impact on Learning.* Abingdon: Routledge.

This book has strongly influenced our thinking, is based on research review evidence and is strongly recommended as worthy of further study. Hattie develops the powerful idea that 'the greatest effects on student learning occur when teachers become learners of their own teaching, and when students become their own teachers' (p 18).

Sternberg, R. J. and Grigorenko, E. L. (2007) *Teaching for Successful Intelligence: To Increase Student Learning and Achievement*. London: Sage.

An accessible and powerful framework for planning lessons and programmes to balance the development of analytical, creative and practical intelligence. We recommend this approach as a way to work towards balance in your impact as a teacher on learning and on learners.

References

Boyd, P. (2014) Learning Teaching in School, in Cooper, H. (ed) *Professional Studies in Primary Education* (2nd edn). London: Sage. Companion website available at: www.uk.sagepub.com/upm-data/61142_Cooper.pdf (accessed 1 May 2015).

Boyd, P., and Bloxham, S. (2014) A Situative Metaphor for Teacher Learning: The Case of University Tutors Learning to Grade Student Coursework. *British Educational Research Journal* 40(2), pp 337–52.

Covey, S. R. (2004) *The 7 Habits of Highly Effective People: Powerful Lessons in Personal Change*. London: Simon & Schuster.

Day, C., Stobart, G., Sammons, P., Kington, A. and Gu, Q. (2007) *Teachers Matter: Connecting Lives, Work and Effectiveness*. Maidenhead: Open University Press.

Esquith, R. (2003) *There Are No Shortcuts*. New York: Anchor Books.

Index